W9-AGN-569

"Evangelicals, long suspicious of tradition, much infatuated with innovation, woke up one day, light-headed and sore-footed, and realized we'd followed Jesus into the wilderness but hadn't packed enough for the journey. Just in the nick of time, Robert Elmer has gathered loaves and fishes from sages ancient and recent and—voila!—come up with a veritable feast, with food to spare. I hope this book finds a wide and hungry audience and that its wisdom becomes our daily portion."

—MARK BUCHANAN, author of *The Rest of God*

Rediscovering
DAILY GRACES

Classic Voices on the
Transforming Power of the Sacraments

Robert Elmer

NAVPRESS®

BRINGING TRUTH TO LIFE

OUR GUARANTEE TO YOU

We believe so strongly in the message of our books that we are making this quality guarantee to you. If for any reason you are disappointed with the content of this book, return the title page to us with your name and address and we will refund to you the list price of the book. To help us serve you better, please briefly describe why you were disappointed. Mail your refund request to: NavPress, P.O. Box 35002, Colorado Springs, CO 80935.

The Navigators is an international Christian organization. Our mission is to advance the gospel of Jesus and His kingdom into the nations through spiritual generations of laborers living and discipling among the lost. We see a vital movement of the gospel, fueled by prevailing prayer, flowing freely through relational networks and out into the nations where workers for the kingdom are next door to everywhere.

NavPress is the publishing ministry of The Navigators. The mission of NavPress is to reach, disciple, and equip people to know Christ and to make Him known by publishing life-related materials that are biblically rooted and culturally relevant. Our vision is to stimulate spiritual transformation through every product we publish.

© 2006 by Robert Elmer

All rights reserved. No part of this publication may be reproduced in any form without written permission from NavPress, P.O. Box 35001, Colorado Springs, CO 80935. www.navpress.com

NAVPRESS, BRINGING TRUTH TO LIFE, and the NAVPRESS logo are registered trademarks of NavPress. Absence of ® in connection with marks of NavPress or other parties does not indicate an absence of registration of those marks.

ISBN 1-57683-853-6

Cover design by DesignWorks/John Hamilton
Cover photo by Corbis/Orion Press
Creative Team: Terry Behimer, Liz Heaney, Debby Weaver, Kathy Mosier, Arvid Wallen, Kathy Guist

Unless otherwise identified, all Scripture quotations in this publication are taken from the HOLY BIBLE: NEW INTERNATIONAL VERSION® (NIV®). Copyright © 1973, 1978, 1984 by International Bible Society. Used by permission of Zondervan Publishing House. All rights reserved. Other versions used include: THE MESSAGE (MSG). Copyright © 1993, 1994, 1995, 1996, 2000, 2001, 2002. Used by permission of NavPress Publishing Group; and the King James Version (KJV).

Published in association with the literary agency of Alive Communications, Inc., 7680 Goddard Street, Suite 200, Colorado Springs, CO 80920 (www.alivecommunications.com).

Elmer, Robert.
  Rediscovering daily graces : classic voices on the transforming power of the sacraments / Robert Elmer.
    p. cm.
  Includes bibliographical references.
  ISBN 1-57683-853-6
  1. Sacraments. I. Title.
  BV800.E47 2006
  234'.46—dc22

                              2006004857

Printed in the United States of America

1 2 3 4 5 6 / 10 09 08 07 06

FOR A FREE CATALOG OF NAVPRESS BOOKS & BIBLE STUDIES,
CALL 1-800-366-7788 (USA) OR 1-800-839-4769 (CANADA)

CONTENTS

PART THREE: GRACE TO LIVE

ACKNOWLEDGMENTS

I'd like to thank the staff at NavPress for their untiring support in this project, as well as their creative input along the way. Special thanks to Terry Behimer, who championed the concept from the start, and to Liz Heaney, who expertly guided the editorial process. But so many others at NavPress have caught the vision for what *Rediscovering Daily Graces* represents: renewal in the church, looking back to our scriptural roots. I especially appreciate their willingness to step out in obedience to God's call, no matter what the risks.

Thanks also to the staff at the Crowell Learning Resource Center, that wonderful library at the Moody Bible Institute in downtown Chicago. Roger Van Oosten, reference and Internet librarian, was especially supportive in allowing me unlimited access to valuable (and old!) archived materials. Thank you.

HAVE WE LOST SOMETHING?

Has the church misplaced something?

For centuries Christians defined cradle-to-grave faith through a framework of rituals called "the sacraments," eventually including baptism, confirmation, communion, reconciliation, prayer for the sick, marriage, and vocation. These were seen as God's direct gifts of grace to his people—aids to navigation through the stormy seas of life.

Today, however, many believers feel like spiritual castaways, with only a vague awareness that the Reformation church might have left something behind in its rush to reinvent itself. So now, finally, *Rediscovering Daily Graces* gives us a new way to test for ourselves the tension between reality and ritual, without compromising our evangelical beliefs. It's a rich tapestry of writings from respected writers such as Charles Spurgeon and Andrew Murray, Martin Luther and Dwight Moody—all updated to today's English. (See also section 7, "Vocation and Christian Service.") As their words once more come alive, they give us concrete strategies to reclaim the best of our spiritual heritage and find our way home.

But first, let's take a step back in history as we agree on what the word *sacrament* means to today's reader. There's some mystery as to how early Christians understood the concept and where they started using the word. In fact, in many English Bible translations, *sacrament* is translated "mystery," which is from a Latin rendering of the Greek. If the concept of sacraments actually came from that linguistic branch, it may have been an attempt to say, "There's real meat and truth behind this ceremony. There's meaning at the core."

Another possibility may be that the word *sacrament* simply emerged from the Latin word *sacramentum*, which means "oath." Roman soldiers gave their sacramentum to serve their commanding officer faithfully. In the Christian context, then, a sacrament might have been taken as a way for believers to pledge their loyalty to our Commander-in-Chief, Jesus.

Either way, the early church began to look at the sacraments as God-given practices that every faithful believer should engage in, though in the earliest years we find little agreement as to the number and scope of the sacraments. It wasn't until about the 1200s that scholars finally began to codify their beliefs as they standardized the number and meaning of the rites.

Several hundred years later, however, Protestant reformers, such as John Calvin and Martin Luther, began to reject much of the mysticism these rites had accumulated—not to mention much of the rest of Rome's theology and practices. From their perspective, the sacraments had moved beyond symbolizing a spiritual truth, taking on a life of their own. In other words, the rites had grown to become not just a *sign* but also a *means* of grace. As a result, the emerging Protestant church largely abandoned the sacraments and all they had ever represented.

With some exceptions. For example, no one disputed that Jesus told his disciples to remember him when they ate bread and drank wine, "in remembrance of me" (Luke 22:19). Even though most Protestants wouldn't agree with the traditional Catholic understanding of the sacrament of communion (the Eucharist), most would say it was somehow special—instituted or modeled by the Lord himself. The same for baptism.

But what of the other sacraments? In addition to the sacraments of communion (the Eucharist) and baptism, the Catholic Church has adopted:

1. *Confirmation.* In Catholic theology, a step augmenting baptism where young people are received fully into the church and empowered for Christian living. Variants on the tradition are practiced by a few Protestant traditions, but the core meaning represents the initial steps of discipleship.
2. *Penance.* In which people confess their sins privately to a priest. Most Protestant denominations largely downplay this practice—or mutual confession in general.
3. *Holy orders.* The solemn dedication of church leadership. In Protestant tradition, pastors and missionaries are ordained or dedicated, though the structure is nowhere near as elaborate.

4. *Matrimony.* Seen as a special commitment before God by both Catholics and Protestants.

5. *Extreme unction.* In which a gravely sick person is prayed over for healing and forgiveness. While beliefs about healing vary widely among evangelical churches, it's still a prominent issue.

In several cases, clear parallels can be drawn between Catholic and Protestant tradition, while in other cases only the root biblical foundation is shared. For example, while Protestants recognize the importance of marriage, asking forgiveness, or dedicated Christian service, they stop short of calling these things "sacraments."

So this book takes a long step backward, perhaps even beyond the roots of the Reformation, on the assumption that each of the practices that grew to become a sacrament had a biblical basis. If so, could it be possible that the Protestant church at some point—in an effort to distance itself from Rome—skipped past an essential element of faith? Or at least a useful teaching?

To find out, we examine the wisdom of Christian thinkers from generations past. For example, what did Luther have to say about communion? Or in more recent times (the late 1800s) what did the beloved South African pastor Andrew Murray write about forgiving one another?

Each excerpt comes from a published work or sermon from years past. Many of the writings are forgotten or out-of-print. But don't let that concern you. To help give the words renewed vibrancy and the impact they might have had on their original audience, I've rendered them from the original wording (sometimes, as in the case of Luther, from translations) to a more contemporary English. My conviction is that reaching new generations with the truth outweighs any of our own sentimental attachments to antique phrasing. As Luther once wrote:

> When we're translating, we shouldn't ask the Latin how we should speak German. Instead we should ask the mother in the home, the children on the street, the common man in the marketplace. We need to look them in the mouth to see how they speak, and afterwards do our translating. That way our readers will understand because we're coming to them in their own mother tongue.
>
> —From Martin Luther, "On Translating:
> An Open Letter," addressed to Wenzel Link
> (Nuremberg, Germany: September 12, 1530)

Clearly *Rediscovering Daily Graces* isn't about German, but Luther had the right idea—making scriptural truth accessible to the people on the street, in a language that makes sense to them. Even though at the time Luther was hounded and criticized by purists, his stubborn dedication helped fuel a revolution that continues to this day. Imagine being able to hear God's words as if he were speaking our own language!

Obviously *Rediscovering Daily Graces* isn't Scripture, but

it's presented here in the tradition of Luther and others who wanted nothing more than to deliver God's truth to as many people as possible. As you read, you may notice some disagreement between writers on shades of meaning or on church practice. One writer may contradict another. But that's okay. It's up to each reader to decide what might apply to his or her own walk with God or church practice.

As you read, then, please take this book as a suggestion for growth, as a spiritual to-do list of sorts. It is nothing if not practical. Remember that we benefit by looking at the root of tradition, then listening to what an earlier generation had to say about its biblical foundations. Let these readings challenge you to rethink your place in God's timeline and God's church.

Finally, I've divided the readings into three parts. Part One, Grace to Begin, includes baptism, confirmation, and communion. Part Two, Grace to Heal, includes reconciliation, and prayer for the sick and hurting. And Part Three, Grace to Live, includes marriage, and vocation and Christian service. Be sure to make full use of the study questions at the end of each of these Christian practices, divided into seven sections. They're designed to help get you started and can be used for individual growth or group study.

—*Robert Elmer*

LIST OF AUTHORS

Tertullian (Quintus Septimius Florens Tertullianus) (c. 155–230) Roman convert to Christianity whose sharp wit and mind helped define the early church's thinking.

Cyril of Jerusalem (c. 315–386) Distinguished theologian and thinker in the early church, ordained as a deacon and as a priest.

Martin Luther (1483–1546) German priest whose "95 Theses" originally called for debate and reform but ignited the Protestant Reformation.

John Calvin (1509–1564) Influential French theologian whose landmark *The Institutes of the Christian Religion* helped change the roadmap of the Reformation.

George Whitefield (1714–1770) Minister and traveling preacher who helped found the Methodist church and whose preaching helped spark revival in the colonies.

John Wesley (1703–1791) British theologian and preacher who, with George Whitefield and his own brother Charles, helped found the Methodist movement.

Søren Aabye Kierkegaard (1813–1855) Danish Christian philosopher whose views on faith and ethics would eventually bring him to world attention.

Charles Grandison Finney (1792–1875) A leader in a rise in evangelicalism that became known as the "Second Great Awakening." His preaching has influenced many, including singer Keith Green and Pastor Billy Graham.

Charles Haddon (C. H.) Spurgeon (1834–1892) British Baptist known as the "Prince of Preachers," whose printed sermons for years have helped define Christian thinking.

Dwight Lyman (D. L.) Moody (1837–1899) The leading evangelist of his day, whose work in Chicago led to the founding of the Moody Bible Institute.

William Booth (1829–1912) Founder and first general of the Salvation Army, along with his wife and coworker Catherine.

Andrew Murray (1828–1917) South African minister in the Dutch Reformed church whose prolific writings on church life and renewal are still popular today.

Albert Benjamin (A. B.) Simpson (1843–1919) Canadian-born preacher and writer whose concern for global evangelism helped form the Christian and Missionary Alliance.

Frederick Brotherton (F. B.) Meyer (1847–1929) British Baptist leader with strong connections to the Keswick holiness and renewal movements, which led to modern-day Pentecostalism.

PART ONE

GRACE
TO BEGIN

BAPTISM

IMAGINE PUTTING CHARLES SPURGEON, Cyril of Jerusalem, Andrew Murray, and Martin Luther in the same room to discuss the subject of baptism in the church. Perhaps Spurgeon, the Baptist evangelist, might have a difficult time finding common ground with Cyril, the early church father. Andrew Murray, who was from a Reformed background, might also disagree with the others. Luther might well write up his theses on the subject, nail them on the wall, and storm out of the room to form his own denomination.

Such disagreements have been raging for hundreds of years. What is it about baptism that raises so many denominational hackles? Because face it—probably no other practice has divided more churches than baptism. Sprinkle or dunk? A symbol, or more than that? For infants, children, or adults? Immediately upon conversion, or later? And why was Jesus himself baptized? What does Jesus really want us to do about baptism, as a church?

Many Christians believe they have found definitive answers

to these questions, answers bound up in their particular interpretation of Scripture. The authors of the excerpts to follow had an opinion or two as well. As we read them, it's up to us to work through our own beliefs—and to decide for ourselves where baptism fits into our personal theology. And then, to determine where it fits into what we believe and practice in our home church. Because there's one part of baptism that nearly every believer can agree upon:

Baptism matters. And because it does matter, we'll take seriously what's been written on the subject, applying it with care.

Chapter 1

THE GOOD ANANIAS

CHARLES SPURGEON

B y their very name, Baptists declare to the world that much of what they believe about salvation centers around the practice of baptism, although we see variation of thought between Southern Baptists, American Baptists, Independent Baptists, General Conference Baptists, and so on. The Reverend Charles Haddon (C. H.) Spurgeon was always a good Baptist. During his ministry he presented the gospel to thousands of people around the world. Of course he told them about being baptized, as Scripture commands. Here's a brief segment of one of his messages on Ananias. Not the Ananias who was struck down for lying about his offering, but Ananias the Syrian believer who obeyed God and placed his hands on Paul to restore the new apostle's sight.

Notice how totally faithful Ananias was. He said to Paul, "Get up, be baptized and wash your sins away, calling on his name" (Acts 22:16). But a lot of evangelists today tend to shy away from the "baptized" part. The main thing, they say, is to get a person saved, to get a person believing on the Lord Jesus Christ, period. Somehow "arise *and be baptized*" doesn't seem as important.

But as for me, I wouldn't dare mess with the clear message of Jesus. I have to deliver it as a package deal—nothing more, nothing less.

Even though people say, "Let's not talk about baptism; it's just a partisan doctrine," I ask, "Who said so?" If our Lord commanded it, who dares call it partisan or sectarian or anything like that? We're not called to preach 94 percent of the gospel, but 100 percent—no matter what's politically correct. Just as Ananias did. Doesn't it say in Mark 16:16 that "whoever believes and is baptized will be saved"? Why leave off some of the words?

I'm even wondering if God is holding back his blessing from some preachers and teachers because they haven't passed along the entire message of Jesus.

Just wait. I'm going to get a letter from a Christian brother saying, "Sorry, but I can't pass along your sermon notes this week since you're getting into a controversial subject like baptism."

Well, dear believer, if you can't distribute this message, I'm going to have to do without your kind help. Because I can't modify God's Word or twist the meaning to please the best person on the planet.

Just look at the text to see how important baptism is! Now, we'd be making a big mistake if we took it to mean that baptism itself saves a person—what's called "baptismal regeneration." The physical washing of water has nothing to do with removing sin from our lives. Still, we're not allowed to put something in the background that Scripture places in the front row.

Ananias said to Paul, "Get up, be baptized and wash your sins away." These words fit well with the words of Jesus in Mark 16, "Whoever believes and is baptized will be saved." In both of these texts, the Lord elevates baptism, giving it a special honor. We'd be making a big mistake to ignore something Jesus obviously believes is important.

So again, don't think for a minute that dunking yourself in water can actually wash away sin. But do remember that if the Lord closely links baptism—an outward testimony—with washing away sins, then this is a big deal to him.

Also remember the text from Romans where Paul assures us that "it is with your heart that you believe and are justified, and it is with your mouth that you confess and are saved" (10:10). Faith has to be followed by obedience; if it's not, that only proves the faith wasn't sincere (and from the heart) to begin with. So do what Jesus asks you to do.

But that's not my point, actually. My point is this: We always need to handle God's Word carefully. We need to be true to what he reveals to us—right down to the minute points, the commas and the periods.

There's a lot of talk these days about not being narrow, exclusive, or denominational. Being nondenominational or ecumenical is cool, and I understand the upside of that. The danger, though, is that we sacrifice bits and pieces of God's

Word for the sake of some imaginary unity. For the sake of that unity we might feel pressured to give up a little bit of doctrine here, or a little there. Hey, it's not really important, right?

Wrong. I'm telling you right now: Never, ever give up anything that your Lord commands. Sure, go ahead and give other believers the benefit of the doubt, imagine that they want to hold on to 100-percent truth, as well. But whether other Christians hold the line or not, you hold on! That's the best way to be nondenominational. Be faithful to what you hold true, hold true to Jesus, and give your brothers and sisters credit for doing the same.

If we do that, we can expect the Master's blessing.

From Charles Spurgeon, "The Good Ananias,
a Lesson for Believers," a sermon delivered at the
Metropolitan Tabernacle (Newington, England, 1885)

Chapter 2

WHAT DO THE SYMBOLS MEAN?

CYRIL OF JERUSALEM

Cyril, the bishop of Jerusalem in 348, lived roughly three centuries after the time of Christ. Like everyone else at the time, he didn't seem to enjoy the advantage of a proper last name, so "of Jerusalem" will have to do. He did have a bit of a stormy church career, but he is most known for writing a complete handbook for baptism candidates, called the Catechetical Lectures. This handbook gives us a good idea of what baptism was like in the fourth century and tells us that adults were commonly baptized at that time. Here's a brief excerpt.

"Don't you know that all of us who were baptized into Christ Jesus were baptized into his death? . . . because you are not under law, but under grace" (Romans 6:3,14).

We're reading daily introductions to God's mysteries, plus

new how-to instructions that announce new truths. These messages help us all, but mostly you, since you've just been turned into a new person in Jesus. So now you're going to learn what all the symbols meant when you were baptized the other day in the inner chamber, the baptism room.

First of all, getting rid of your street clothes was like putting away the old person you used to be, a person stained by sin. Remember Jesus left his clothes behind, too, when he was on the cross. From now on you won't be wearing those clothes any more—and I'm not talking about your physical clothes. I'm talking about the person you once were and will never be again.

After all the preparations, you were led to the baptismal pool. This reminds us of how Jesus was carried from the cross to the tomb. You were asked if you believed in God the Father, Son, and Holy Spirit, and you said you did. Then they took you down into the water—down three times and up three times, which is a symbol of how Christ was buried three days. Going down was like Jesus going down into the heart of the earth. You couldn't see anything as you went down, but when you came back up, you could open your eyes—as if you were coming back up into the day. You were dying and being born, all at the same time, and this salvation water was like a grave and your mother, all at once. Remember what Solomon said in Ecclesiastes 3:2: "a time to be born and a time to die." Only in your case, in reverse: a time to die and a time to be born. Both at the same time; your birth went hand in hand with your death.

From Cyril of Jerusalem, *Mystagogical Catechesis 2.2,*
Catechetical Lectures (c. 350)

Chapter 3

THE DOOR
TO A COVENANT

ANDREW MURRAY

*A*ndrew Murray is considered one of the finest devotional *writers of his time. And even today thousands of Christians read his descriptions of the deeper life in Christ. In this excerpt he reveals no less devotion, even as he describes his dedication to a distinctly Reformed outlook on baptism. After all, Murray was ordained in the Dutch Reformed denomination.*

"Therefore go and make disciples of all nations, baptizing them in the name of the Father and of the Son and of the Holy Spirit, and teaching them to obey everything I have commanded you" (Matthew 28:19-20).

"Whoever believes and is baptized will be saved, but whoever does not believe will be condemned" (Mark 16:16).

These two verses sum up the meaning of baptism. In

the verse from Matthew's gospel the word *teach* means "make disciples of all nations, baptizing them." As believing disciples are baptized in water, they are also to be baptized or introduced into the name of the Three-One God. In the name of the Father we're showered with new birth and life as a child in the love of the Father. In the name of the Son we're forgiven of our sins and given life in Christ. In the name of the Holy Spirit we receive day-by-day renewal and the indwelling of that same Spirit.

So every baptized believer must look at baptism as the door to a covenant with the Three-One God. Baptism is a pledge from God that the Father, Son, and Spirit will do what God has promised every believer. Coming to know every blessing of baptism is a lifelong study.

Other Scriptures also describe the blessing, which is intertwined with the new birth that produces a child of God. John 3:5 says that "no one can enter the kingdom of God unless he is born of water and the Spirit." So baptized disciples have to live like children in the love of God, their Father.

Other passages link baptism even more closely with our redemption in Christ. At its core, baptism represents forgiveness—the washing away of sins. Since forgiveness is always the gateway to blessing, baptism symbolizes the beginning of our Christian walk, but with one difference: It's a beginning that stays with us always.

With this in mind, we see in Romans 6 that baptism is the secret to a holy walk with the Lord, as well as a jumping-off point for being one with him. Paul asks, "Don't you know that all of us who were baptized into Christ Jesus were baptized into his death?" After that he goes into more detail about what that really means, and how we arise out of such a baptism into new life in Jesus.

This idea can be boiled down to one powerful verse: "All of you who were baptized into Christ have clothed yourselves with Christ" (Galatians 3:27). Baptism basically describes the life of a disciple: someone who is clothed with Christ. Just as a person is plunged beneath the water in baptism, so the believer is baptized into Christ's death. This baptism is the first step in living and walking, clothed with the new life of Jesus.

Other Bible passages connect baptism with the promise of the Spirit—not only the spirit of new life (the way we've already seen), but the Spirit God gives believers as a seal. The Spirit that will live in believers to renew them day-by-day. Look at Titus 3:5-6, where it says, "He saved us through the washing of rebirth and renewal by the Holy Spirit, whom he poured out on us generously." In other words, the Spirit of God renews us, since the new life planted in us soaks through our being to the point where everything we think and do is flavored by God's high, holy standards.

We say "yes" in faith to all these rich blessings, poured out on us through baptism. After all, Mark 16:16 reminds us that "whoever believes and is baptized will be saved." So baptism isn't just a way of confessing the faith we already own; it's also a sign from God. It's his way of sealing the deal, his way of opening up the treasury of grace and keeping it open for the disciple to draw on for a lifetime.

Remember, the believing candidate for baptism is baptized

into the death of Christ. He or she will be "wearing" Jesus from now on, with daily help from the Holy Spirit. So every time a baptized believer sees another baptism (or thinks once more on it), it's an encouragement to press on into the full salvation life God has prepared. In the process, God gives us his Spirit to gather up all the Father's love and the Son's grace.

> Lord God, please anchor your holy baptism in my soul, always reminding me that I'm baptized into the death of Christ. Open the eyes and the hearts of your people everywhere to understand and experience the rich blessing open in the baptism of their children. Amen.

> From Andrew Murray, *The New Life: Words of God for Young Disciples of Christ* (New York: Hurst & Co., 1891)

Chapter 4

LUTHER ON BAPTISM

MARTIN LUTHER

No one usually said it more plainly than did Martin Luther. This leader of the Reformation church never shrank from stepping on toes or striking out at his opponents—even if he offended people in the process. No—Luther wore his heart (and his opinions) on his sleeve, and he worked hard to express himself in books, pamphlets, and sermons. In this excerpt, Luther takes his gloves off and tells it as he sees it.

In Greek, the word for "baptism" is *baptismos*, while in Latin it's *mersio*, which means to plunge something entirely underwater, so the water closes over it. Today in many churches it's no longer the custom to plunge children into the baptismal, but only to take a little water from the font and pour it over them. Even so, immersion is what should be done. It would be right, according to the meaning of the word, that the child (or whoever is baptized) should be sunk totally under the water and pulled out again. Because even in German the word for baptism, *taufe*, surely comes from the word *tief*, which means that what is baptized is sunk deeply into the water. The significance of baptism also calls us to understand the word in this way because baptism is a symbol of how God's grace completely drowned the old sinful person. That's why we should do justice to the real meaning of the word and make baptism a true and complete sign of the thing it symbolizes.

From Martin Luther, "A Treatise on Baptism" (November 1519)

✼

Chapter 5

TRANSLATING BAPTISM

MARTIN LUTHER

Once again Martin Luther lays it on the line, giving specific instructions both to those who would be baptized and to those who would do the baptizing. Note that Luther has an endearing way of stripping down all the fluff and getting to the meat of his message.

I hear every day how many children are being baptized by priests who hardly seem to care and witnessed by people who don't understand what's going on. What should be a solemn, special occasion is being ruined! So I recommend from now on that we conduct baptisms in German rather than Latin. That's what I'm doing. That way, sponsors and others will be able to catch a better vision of what's going on, and this will help build their faith and devotion to the Lord. It will also be easier for priests to plug into the ceremony with more concern for those they're serving.

As a believer I want everyone who has a part in baptism to understand what it's all about—including the serious and solemn side of it. Just for example, if witnesses to a baptism could understand one of the baptism prayers, they'd see how important young people are in the church. They'd understand the hold of Satan on our lives before we're saved, how we're children of sin. They'd also be able to pray for God's favor and grace through baptism—that these young people would become children of God.

Don't forget it's no joke to side up against Satan; it's no small thing to drive the Devil away from these kids. By doing so, we're loading on very young shoulders a crafty, lifelong enemy. Remember also that we need to stand behind these young people with all our faith and all our heart. We need to pray for them, asking God both to free them from the power of the Devil and to strengthen them so they can resist Satan like a true Christian knight. I'm thinking the reason so many young people fall away after baptism is because we don't pray for them seriously or enough.

Here's another thing to remember: In baptism the ceremonial stuff matters the least. I'm talking about things such as signing with the cross, wearing special christening robes, holding baptismal candles, or any other custom people have dreamed up to beautify the ceremony. We can baptize a person without all these things. Besides, they don't do much to scare off the Devil. He sneers at more impressive things than these! Instead, we need dedicated hearts that look first to please God.

Concentrate on this instead: Come to the ceremony in

true faith, believing the promises of God. Listen to God's Word carefully when it's read. Follow along from the heart during group prayer. After all, that's what the priest means when he says, "Let us pray," isn't it? Sponsors and everyone else should repeat every word of the prayer in their hearts, while prayer leaders should keep the prayer clear and slow so people can follow along. The idea is to hold up the young person before God's throne and stand against the Devil on the child's behalf, in the name of Jesus. Because as far as the Devil is concerned, this is a big deal!

From Martin Luther, "Martin Luther to All Christian Readers,"
in *The Order of Baptism* (Wittenberg, Germany, 1523)

PUTTING THE WORDS TO WORK

QUESTIONS FOR INDIVIDUAL
OR GROUP STUDY

Use these questions as springboards for individual or group study.

1. Describe the tension Charles Spurgeon felt between being ecumenical (reaching out to believers of other Christian traditions) and holding true to Scripture as he understood it. (See "The Good Ananias.") How can you turn that tension into a balance in your Christian walk and your relationships with other believers?

2. Read "The Good Ananias" again. Are there any times when you would prefer to keep quiet on doctrinal issues for the sake of unity? When would you keep quiet, and when would you not . . . and why?

3. Spurgeon delivered his "Good Ananias" sermon in 1885. How does his description of how evangelists in the late

nineteenth century treated baptism compare to how we treat it today? How can we apply this to our own practice?

4. Read Cyril of Jerusalem's description of fourth-century baptism. Is there anything they did back then that you think could be more emphasized today in your own church? Any of his practices you could follow? What would happen if you did?

5. In "The Door to a Covenant," Andrew Murray mentions being "clothed" with Christ. What do those clothes look like in your life? How are they worn, and what do they do?

6. Do you agree that Andrew Murray seems to believe baptism is more than just a symbol? If you were to agree with him, how might that change the way you view or practice baptism? If you don't agree with him, why not?

7. Today's Lutherans practice infant baptism by sprinkling. Were you surprised by what Luther said about the original meaning of baptism? (See "Luther on Baptism.") How important do you think it might be to look back at the original Greek or Hebrew meaning to understand your own view of a practice? Do you think it's important to understand the original, intended meaning?

8. Have you ever attended a church ceremony where you didn't understand what was really going on? How did that make you feel? In light of that, what do you think of Luther's advice on prayer during baptism? (See "Translating Baptism.") If you were going to follow his teaching, how might that affect your own worship?

9. Have you ever been uncomfortable when someone talked

about the influence of the Devil? Do you think Luther places more of an emphasis on spiritual warfare and the influence of Satan than we do in today's church? (See "Translating Baptism.") How do you think his view of Satan compares with that of Jesus, and with your own?

10. Read "Luther on Baptism" and "Translating Baptism" once more. If you saw the world more like Luther, would that change the way you lived out your faith? In what way? Is there anything in his approach to spirituality that you would adopt?

CONFIRMATION

CATHOLICS GENERALLY BELIEVE THAT by means of confirmation, young Christians are clothed with the seven gifts of the Spirit—wisdom, understanding, counsel, fortitude, knowledge, piety, and the fear of the Lord. They hold confirmation in high esteem as a sacrament given directly by God for the use and building up of the church.

A portion of this doctrine is not controversial among non-Catholics. Nearly all Christians would agree that young Christians would benefit from such gifts. But Protestants don't generally assign a mystical quality to the coming-of-age ceremony, even if they do practice a variation of confirmation. In many cases confirmation in a Protestant church is simply a milestone ceremony whereby young tweens of twelve or thirteen years old are initiated into church membership after a period of training and instruction in church history and doctrinal distinctives. Young people who go through a confirmation program should know something of what their church believes, and this is generally the goal of non-Catholic confirmation programs today.

Lutherans, in particular, have held tightly to the custom and practice of confirmation. Yet it's interesting that Martin Luther himself had little good to say about it:

> In particular, avoid that monkey business, confirmation, which is really a fanciful deception. I would permit confirmation as long as it is understood that God knows nothing of it, and has said nothing about it, and that what the bishops claim for it is untrue. They mock our God when they say that it is one of God's sacraments, for it is purely human contrivance.
>
> —From Martin Luther, *The Estate of Marriage*,
> part 1 (Wittenberg, Germany, 1522)

Most of the other reformers would have agreed with Luther in his views about confirmation as it was practiced then, and so would many of today's Protestant leaders and teachers. Perhaps that's why so few evangelical churches today practice confirmation. But if we back up several steps from the controversy, we might recognize the biblical roots of this sacrament; we might see what makes this practice a graceful gift of God—or at least one that could help strengthen the church. As such, we can select the root that, if planted and watered, could once again grow to become useful.

We start by stripping the idea of confirmation down to its original, unassuming, biblical basis, which could very well be the apostle Paul's admonition for believers to "study to shew thyself approved unto God" (2 Timothy 2:15, KJV). This popular verse is often used as a basis for a number of Christian education programs, from Sunday schools to midweek Awana youth programs to vacation Bible school.

So if we begin with the understanding that traditional confirmation is nothing more than the formal biblical training of young people for the purpose of lifetime service, we realize what this grace of God really is, at its core:

Discipleship with a graduation ceremony.

Chapter 6

TRUE CONFIRMATION

JOHN CALVIN

Today a portion of the Protestant church still follows John Calvin's teachings and his view of God's sovereignty. Though he grew up in France, Calvin made his theological mark among the reformers in both France and Switzerland. Often stormy and insistent, Calvin made his share of enemies. He also wrote the highly influential The Institutes of the Christian Religion, *in which he had much to say about just about everything—including confirmation.*

Christians in ancient times had a custom of bringing their older children to the local bishop for confirmation. This ceremony completed a duty rooted in the baptism of those grown children years ago. But before the confirmation could take place, these young people had to learn the basics of what they believed. That done, they would confess their faith in front of the bishop and the rest of the church. These children obviously couldn't do this when they were baptized as infants, so the confirmation ceremony allowed the bishop to see if they could express their faith as adolescents. To give this holy ceremony more reverence and dignity, the bishop would lay his hands on the young person being confirmed. This was simply a solemn blessing.

Ancient writers and church leaders such as Pope Leo and Jerome often mentioned the ceremony. Jerome said that bishops gave their blessing as a sign of honor—not because they had to or because there was any magic to it. While I don't agree with Jerome about everything, I think if we take confirmation that way—simply as a symbol of blessing—we can and should use this part of the ceremony once again.

I wish we could keep the custom of confirmation, the way Christians did in the early church before it was turned into a sacrament. We wouldn't treat confirmation the way some do, adding on layers of mystic beliefs that aren't in the Bible and that tend to pollute a clear understanding of biblical baptism. We would simply take young people and have them stand up and explain their faith to the rest of the church. We'd come up with lesson plans that would explain the basics of what we believe as Christians, the kinds of things everyone would agree on. Then we'd simply quiz the ten-year-olds who were coming up through the confirmation class. If they didn't know something, or understand it, they'd be taught. This way we'd all witness young children explaining and testifying our one true faith, with which we worship the one true God.

If we had this kind of program in place, it would motivate those parents who had a tough time teaching their kids at home. It would strengthen everyone's faith, bringing up the level of awareness several notches. It would also help inoculate us against loose or unorthodox doctrine, even as it would help us all to plug the truth of the gospel into our thoughts and lives in a more powerful and organized way.

From John Calvin, *The Institutes of the Christian Religion*, chapter 19 (1559), trans. Henry Beveridge, *Calvin's Institutes* (Grand Rapids, MI: Christian Classics Ethereal Library, 1845)

Chapter 7

DON'T HOLD KIDS BACK

CHARLES SPURGEON

*S*ociety in the eighteenth and nineteenth centuries had little room
or patience for children. That's why Charles Spurgeon's landmark book Come, Ye Children was so unusual. In it, he came
out as a strong advocate for young people—and for the dignity and
high worth of those who would work with them. Through orphanages
and with simple, straightforward teaching, his ministry was in large
part built on outreach to younger people. The book's subtitle, "A Book
for Parents and Teachers on the Christian Training of Children," gave
adults with hearts for kids a strong dose of encouragement. Here's a
selection from Spurgeon's message.

It's a sin for parents to overlook their children's spiritual education. Maybe they think that young kids don't have enough
spiritual understanding to become Christians at an early age.
As a result, they don't seem to care what kind of education
children receive.

Yet even though it does matter, too many parents still don't seem to notice or care, even as the child is moving on to higher education. So parents send their children away to colleges and universities for a prestigious degree, to schools full of moral and spiritual booby traps. I see it time after time: The graduates return with zero morals, their faith shipwrecked.

We reap what we sow. So let's expect more of our children. Let's expect them to know the Lord. Let's introduce them to Jesus as we teach them their ABCs. Let them read their first lessons from the Bible. It's amazing how quickly kids learn to read from the New Testament, and there's something in it that attracts even the youngest readers.

As parents, let's never be guilty of forgetting our children's spiritual training. If we do forget, we may be guilty of the blood of their souls.

Even in our churches, sometimes teachers don't expect children to make genuine commitments to Christ. The theory is that we're doing fine if we just expose the kids to spiritual truth, and that in a few years (after they're more mature) they'll be in a better position to make a real, lasting decision. We sometimes don't expect young children to make valid decisions to follow Christ. When they say they do, we pat them on the head and think it's cute, but in the back of our minds we're thinking a child's decision is not on the same level as an adult commitment. In other words, young children who accept Christ . . . well, it's a little absurd.

I cling to that "absurdity" with all my heart. I believe that the kingdom of God belongs to such children, both here on earth and in heaven. So even if adults don't accept a very young child's profession of faith, I do. Yes, I agree that all new converts should be carefully examined before they're baptized and admitted into the church. I just don't agree that the very young should be automatically excluded most of the time.

From Charles Spurgeon, *Come, Ye Children,* chapter 2
(London: Passmore & Alabaster, 1897)

Chapter 8

THE PSALMIST'S INVITATION

CHARLES SPURGEON

t's hard to miss the high regard Pastor Charles Spurgeon held for children and the high respect he had for their spiritual understanding. Of course, he and his wife, Susannah, had twin sons (who both went on to become preachers, as well!), and the Spurgeons were instrumental in founding a well-known orphanage. Here's an even clearer statement of his belief and interest in young people, taken from his unusual book Come, Ye Children.

"Come, my children, listen to me; I will teach you the fear of the LORD" (Psalm 34:11).

The Bible doctrine here is that children are capable of being taught to honor, respect, and love the Lord. Here's how that works. . . .

First, remember that people generally appear the most

wise after they've acted most foolishly. For example, David in the Bible had acted extremely foolishly before growing truly wise. In his later wisdom he probably wouldn't express foolish ideas or give foolish advice. Keep that in mind.

Now, some people say that children can't understand the deepest parts of our faith. I've even known some Sunday school teachers who just stuck to the basics and held back from teaching kids many of the greater truths of the gospel. They believed their students couldn't handle it! That's a shame.

Yet even some preachers make the same mistake; they don't teach certain biblical doctrines in the mistaken belief that people will not get it, or they'll stumble over the truth. Give me a break! If God has revealed it, we should be preaching it. As long as it's from God's Word, even if I don't quite get it, I will still preach and believe it. The bottom line is that if children are ready to be saved, they're ready to hear any doctrine from God's Word. No exceptions. I would teach kids all the great truths, and they'll be able to build on them the rest of their lives.

I'll tell you this: Children *can* understand the Bible. When I was young, I could have discussed all kinds of theological points, since I heard my father's friends talking about that sort of thing all the time. In fact, I think kids can understand some things early on that we can hardly understand later. That's because of their simple faith, and simple faith is just as good as the highest know-how. I hardly know if there's much difference.

If you accept things as a simple child would, you'll often have ideas that escape so-called advanced thinkers. If you really want to know how much kids can learn, just look at many of the kids in our churches and Christian homes. I'm not talking about prodigies or child geniuses, just boys and girls like young Timothy or Samuel in Scripture. Kids who know the Savior's love.

Remember this: As soon as children can be lost, they can be saved. As soon as they can sin, they can believe and accept God's Word—assuming God graciously helps them. As soon as children can learn evil, you'd better believe the Holy Spirit can teach them good. Teachers, don't ever assume your young students won't be able to understand you. If they don't get it, there's a good chance you don't really get it, either. If they're not getting the point, maybe it's your fault. Try simpler words, and you may discover it wasn't their fault.

Young kids can be saved! If the all-powerful God can rescue a gray-haired sinner, he can do the same for a little child. The same God who finds people standing around the marketplace near the end of the day and puts them to work (remember the parable?) calls folks to work for him at dawn. If God can change a mighty river's course, he can steer a newborn trickle. He can do anything—and he can work on a child's heart any way he wants, because everyone is under his command.

I won't go on about this, since I think everyone would agree. But even though many believe that children can be saved, they don't look for it to really happen. In all kinds of churches, adults are put off by kids who seem a little too serious about their faith. Frankly, we're somewhat scared to hear that a little boy loves Jesus too much. Or if we hear of a young girl making a deep commitment to Christ, we write it off as, well, she's just a kid.

Please don't be so suspicious of a child's genuine faith. It's a gentle package we must handle with care. Believe that even the youngest child can be saved, just as much as you can be. So when you see a child come to Jesus, don't doubt it and don't say, "She's only a kid." Never say anything that would offend one of these little ones who believe in Jesus. I pray that God would enable his people to firmly believe that these little buds of grace are worth the best of tender care!

In the end, we need to spiritually feed young people because they're most likely to be overlooked. I'm afraid some of our sermons go over the heads of younger people, even though children are just as much true Christians as all the older people. God will bless you if you can deliver your message so that kids can understand you! And teachers, you'll also be blessed if you think like a young girl so that when you speak to girls, the truth from your heart will flow directly to the hearts of the children.

From Charles Spurgeon, *Come, Ye Children*,
chapter 14, last paragraph from chapter 1
(London: Passmore & Alabaster, 1897)

Chapter 9

CONFIRMED . . .
AND JUSTIFIED

CHARLES SPURGEON

How do we stand before God? Charles Spurgeon wanted to answer that question as he opened his Bible one December morning in front of his Metropolitan Tabernacle congregation. He was well into a series of sermons on the life of Abram (Abraham), who would provide the perfect example. Notice, though, how his thoughts fit right into the idea of confirmation and the grace of Bible training, or discipleship, for young people. Here's an excerpt from a sermon in that series.

Abram didn't obey a set of ceremonial laws to gain God's blessing, and God didn't give Abram his stamp of approval because the man followed a deeper set of moral laws, either. The Bible clearly points out that Abram was justified—that he had God's blessing—*before* he was circumcised. See, he hadn't yet taken the first step into a visible covenant with God, and he hadn't yet taken part in any ceremonies. Yet he was totally, perfectly justified. God called it good, called Abram his own. So anything that happened after that point couldn't add anything to the done deal, since it was already perfect as is. Abram couldn't say that his standing before God had anything to do with the physical act of being circumcised.

We know that much from reading the Bible account. So if you and I want to gain the same standing before God, if we want to be justified like Abram, two things are clear:

First, we can't make our way to God by following some kind of moral code or by being nice people.

Second, God doesn't accept us because we follow some kind of ceremonial script to the letter. Not the ancient sacred ritual we read about in the Old Testament, and not the ritual born from Christian tradition. Neither one will work.

If we're going to be justified before God Abram-style, as Abram's children, it's not going to happen through rites or ceremonies.

So listen very carefully: Baptism is a beautiful thing, but it won't justify or help justify us.

Confirmation was dreamed up by people, not by God. Even if God had commanded it (which he didn't), confirmation wouldn't justify us either.

And even though Jesus established the Lord's supper, it doesn't have any effect on whether God accepts us or not, or how we ultimately stand before him.

Abram had no ceremonies to lean on, but the Bible says

his faith made him righteous. Only his faith! That's the only thing you or I have if we ever want to stand right before God. Remember, God counted Abram as righteous only because of his faith. Faith — first, last, and that's it. There are other Scripture accounts where Abram's faith led to good works, but not in the earlier case. God told him to look up at the stars and said "so shall your offspring be" (Genesis 15:5). And Abram did what? He believed the promise — that was all. This is before he offered his famous sacrifice, before he'd said any holy words, before he'd done anything, anywhere. But what does Scripture say immediately after this?

"Abram believed the LORD, and he credited it to him as righteousness" (Genesis 15:6).

So we should always note the difference between the truth (that living faith produces works) and the lie (that faith and works somehow cooperate to justify us). The only way we become righteous is by believing what Jesus has done for us. The natural by-product of that true faith is clean, holy living. But God won't accept us because of that lifestyle or because of what we do, but simply because we believe his promise. That's why it says in the book of Romans:

> "Abraham was declared fit before God by trusting God to set him right." But it's not just Abraham; it's also us! The same thing gets said about us when we embrace and believe the One who brought Jesus to life when the conditions were equally hopeless.

The sacrificed Jesus made us fit for God, set us right with God. (Romans 4:22-25, MSG)

From Charles Spurgeon, "Justification by Faith,"
a sermon delivered at the Metropolitan Tabernacle
(Newington, England, December 6, 1868)

Chapter 10

KEEP IT SIMPLE

MARTIN LUTHER

Though Martin Luther lends his name to an entire branch *of the Protestant church, and he was a prolific writer, he is perhaps best known for putting together two modest works, the Larger Catechism and the Small Catechism. In them, he puts forth what he believes to be the basics of the Christian faith, and in so doing he laid out a pattern of belief and practice that has influenced many generations of young Christians, in and out of the Lutheran denomination. In the preface, he explains even further what he is trying to accomplish.*

I've designed and put together this message to teach children and others who like their theology simple. Our word *catechism* comes from the ancient Greek, a word that has come to mean the basics, what every Christian needs to know. Those who do not know these basics shouldn't participate fully in the life of the church, particularly in ceremonies such as baptism or communion. In the same way professionals such as mechanics need to know their craft—or they should quit. So young Christians should learn this catechism well—and put it to use in their lives.

It's also an adult's duty every week to check with his children and with those who work for him. Do they know this material, or are they learning it? If not, he should keep them to it. Otherwise they'll turn out like the people I meet almost daily—rude, old people who don't know anything about their faith. They ought to know better. Even so, these people are still baptized and attend communion services.

Most people would do well to know the three basic parts of this catechism: the Ten Commandments, the Apostles' Creed, and the Lord's Prayer. Our children should be able to recite them in the morning when they wake, as well as when they sit down to eat. Once they learn these basics, they should learn the Scriptures that have to do with baptism, such as Matthew 28:19 and following, and Mark 16:15-16.

Yet it's not enough to just learn and repeat the words. Young people should also be required to listen to their church's sermon, especially when the preacher is talking about the points in the catechism. If they listen carefully, they'll be able to understand the basis for their faith, and they'll be able to answer any questions if asked.

That's why we put so much weight on preaching the catechism, not in ways people won't be able to understand, but briefly and with a totally simple approach. We want these truths to find a permanent place in the listeners' hearts and minds.

From Martin Luther, "Short Preface of Dr. Martin Luther,"
Luther's Small Catechism (Wittenberg, Germany, 1529)

PUTTING THE WORDS TO WORK

QUESTIONS FOR INDIVIDUAL OR GROUP STUDY

Use these questions as springboards for individual or group study.

1. What did John Calvin wish about confirmation? (See "True Confirmation.") What advantages does he cite for his proposal? Do any of these advantages still apply today?

2. How are Calvin's views on confirmation different from (or similar to) your own? Upon which Scriptures would you base your preferences?

3. Charles Spurgeon was obviously angry at the way some parents sent their kids off to secular schools, only to lose their faith. (See "Don't Hold Kids Back.") If Spurgeon were alive today, what kind of school situations do you think would make him angry? Do you share Spurgeon's concern? Why, or why not?

4. Describe Spurgeon's philosophy of Christian education as it applies to young children. If he were your church's CE director, what kind of program do you think he would put into place?

5. According to Spurgeon, what are some of the worst mistakes a teacher can make? (See "The Psalmist's Invitation.") As a teacher, how would you avoid those mistakes?

6. Look at what Spurgeon says about children in "The Psalmist's Invitation." Have you ever wondered how much a young child really understood about the Lord? How old do you think a child must be before that child can make a serious spiritual commitment? Defend your position.

7. Do you agree with Spurgeon when he says that "confirmation was dreamed up by people, not by God?" (See "Confirmed . . . and Justified.") Explain why or why not. Even if a practice is dreamed up by people, can it still honor God? How?

8. In "Keep It Simple" Martin Luther seems to place a lot of emphasis on memorizing both Scripture and creeds. Why do you think he does this? Explain some of the pros—and cons—of this kind of learning.

9. Luther also talks about a parent's responsibilities to follow up on a child's learning progress. Do you agree with him on this point? If so, what are some creative ways to involve parents in their children's spiritual training?

10. Based on what you've read from Calvin, Spurgeon, and Luther, list the top three qualities of an effective confirmation or Christian education program.

Section Three

COMMUNION

BECAUSE THE ACCOUNT OF the Lord's supper is written so plainly in Scripture, virtually no Christian tradition denies the unique place of this ceremony in the life of the church. Jesus asked that we remember him by this meal—and so we do. He asks that we take and eat—and so we do. He asks that we continue this celebration—and so we do.

The challenge comes when Christians try to decide what this wonderful supper really means. Ironically, for a ceremony that was intended to foster unity among followers of Christ, there's been enough disagreement over communion through the years to bring about far too many congregational splits.

So we look at this simple supper once again, prayerfully asking that God would reveal to us what he really intended. Perhaps we've got it wrong, perhaps we need to reexamine our most deeply guarded traditions in favor of the truth of the Bible. Maybe these writers from past generations have something fresh and new to say to our church today—even if we don't fully agree with them.

Chapter II

THE DIVINE INVITATION

ANDREW MURRAY

*S*ome of Andrew Murray's finest devotional writings describe *communion with Jesus—and not just in the wine and the bread, but knowing God and knowing him more intimately. More than nearly anyone else in his generation, Murray gave us a look at the way things could be. Here's a word of encouragement from the South African-born preacher.*

"Everything is ready. Come to the wedding banquet" (Matthew 22:4).

Listen well to the King of the universe: In honor of his Son he's prepared you a great feast. When you get there you're going to see Jesus, looking great and wonderful—and like one of us. You're going to see all the other believers that the Father loves. He's invited them to this great Love Fest, and he's ready to welcome them as honored guests . . . and friends. He's going to lay out a spread of heaven's best food, but that's just the start of all the great gifts that will come with the life that never ends.

Did you notice the return address on your invitation? Heaven! Can you believe it? The King of glory has asked you to dinner. So you'd better grab this special honor and hold on tight, because it's much more than just your ordinary feast. You'd better concentrate on dressing your best, being on your best behavior, saying the right thing . . . everything that's expected of a guest in the court of the King of kings.

What an amazing invitation! First I think of the banquet and how much it cost God to put it on. If he'd been looking to feed a crew of angels, he needed only to say the word. But a banquet for sin-cursed people on this sin-cursed planet? Now there's a hefty dinner tab. It cost him nothing less than the lifeblood of his Son to cancel the curse and open up the doors to heaven, along with full membership privileges. Nothing less than the body and blood of God's Son would give life to a lost race of people. Just think for a minute on how amazing this King's banquet really is.

I'm thinking of the *invitation,* which is free and open to all. Remember the prophet Isaiah's words? "Come, all you who are thirsty, come to the waters; and you who have no money, come, buy and eat! Come, buy wine and milk without money and without cost" (Isaiah 55:1). Even the most down-and-out and poor have been handed this heartfelt, urgent invitation. The love behind it all springs straight from the Father's heart—this love that has pursued us while we were still sinners, and that stoops to set a table of blessings for us.

I'm thinking of the *blessing* of the banquet. Imagine — dying people will feed from heaven's life-giving entrees, while the lost are rescued and brought back to the address where they really belong, in God's house. Anyone who's thirsty for the Lord will have his or her thirst quenched by God himself, by his love.

Yes, what an amazing invitation! I'll accept it with praise on my lips, even as I get myself ready to attend. I've read about people who offered only excuses and bowed out — one had too much stuff to worry about, another was caught up in job worries, and yet another had family issues. I've heard the voice that said "not one of those originally invited is going to get so much as a bite at my dinner party" (Luke 14:24, MSG).

But I'm convicted that the Holy One has invited me to dinner, and he's not going to stand by and be mocked by his creation. I'm going to focus on him and turn away from the world's undertow so I can yield in obedience to the voice of heavenly love. I'm going to keep company and pray quietly with God's other children so I can stay clear of too much worry about everyday life. I know God himself will help me in this. As an invited guest, I want to meet my God with real hunger and quiet joy.

From Andrew Murray, *The Lord's Table*
(Grand Rapids, MI: Revell, 1897)

Chapter 12

THE LORD'S SUPPER

F. B. MEYER

Frederick Brotherton (F. B.) Meyer was a London-based Baptist evangelist with a deep interest in growing a more holy lifestyle and an abiding concern for addressing the social ills of his day—including prostitution, violence, and drunkenness. The author of more than seventy books, Meyer preached around the world. His big-picture viewpoint shines right through when he starts talking about the Lord's supper.

Believers who love the Lord Jesus can look at the Lord's supper several ways.

Some call it a *Eucharist*—a time of joy and thanksgiving. We see this especially in the early church, when Christians celebrated with laughing and with songs. Let the festival begin! Back then you would never have seen any of the gloom and mystery that have crept into the ceremony.

At the same time, these believers had a clear sense of how

the Lord had conquered death, and they knew exactly how Jesus had suffered, how he would come to life, and how he had opened the gates of heaven to all who believe.

It really says something about our own faith if we can celebrate the same way, with our joy set free to worship.

With others, the Lord's supper is a *sacrament*—an oath. Way back when the city-states of Rome and Carthage competed against each other for power, the mother of a young man named Hannibal brought him to a Roman pagan altar and made him swear he'd always oppose the other city. We can read our history books to see how he honored that oath—in Latin, that *sacramentum.*

In much the same way, we should renew our own *sacramentum* when approaching our Lord's table. We offer ourselves—our souls and our bodies—as a sacrifice to the Lord. We humbly ask that God will fill us to overflowing with a very real sense of his loving hand on our lives.

With others it is a *holy communion.* As Paul asked the Corinthian believers, "When we drink the cup of blessing, aren't we taking into ourselves the blood, the very life, of Christ? And isn't it the same with the loaf of bread we break and eat? Don't we take into ourselves the body, the very life, of Christ?" (1 Corinthians, 10:16, MSG).

There's really only one answer to Paul's question:

Of course.

Without a doubt, the communion service did more to bring together Christians than even the most passionate appeals. Sermons couldn't do it. Back then, people knew that

Jesus himself had invited them to his table, and they wouldn't dare drag along the baggage of racism, national jealousy, or social pride. Everybody who came to the table was just a guest and friend of Jesus, period. Whether they were Jewish or not, Greek or not, master or slave—they forgot who they were as they enjoyed the blessings inside the big tent of Jesus.

Today we need to remember that in the special, even sacred, moment when we eat the bread and drink of the cup, we don't just show our oneness with the people sitting around us. We're also saying we're one with everyone else who confesses Jesus Christ and who observes the same ceremony. Not to mention all the believers who have gone before us! When we celebrate this ceremony-beyond-time, we're as close as we can get to all our fellow believers in heaven and here on earth! This tree of life gives fruit for all of God's family.

With others it's a proclamation, a way to confess to the world what we believe. With this ceremony we remember the heart and soul of our faith. Not the wonderful teachings or the miracles or even that God became man. No. This ceremony announces his death!

Obviously, we also celebrate Christ's coming back to life, just as his disciples did. And speaking of disciples, no one would have celebrated such shame—the horror Jesus went through, the way he seemed to fail—unless it had all been turned on its head by his wonderful victory over death.

Finally, we can also see the Lord's supper as a *sign and seal of the covenant.* You'll notice the concept of covenant clearly included in every gospel account where the supper is described. Jesus said, "This is my blood of the covenant, which is poured out for many" (Mark 14:24; Matthew 26:28; see also Luke 22:20).

In the Old Testament, the Tree of Life was Adam's sign of the Eden covenant. God gave Noah a rainbow as a sign that he would not again destroy the earth with a flood. Abraham received a sign in circumcision, while Israel got the Passover meal.

Now the Lord's supper is our sign of the new covenant God made with us through Jesus. In this supper, God shows how he's our God and we're his people. He shows how he puts away our sins and gives us the Holy Spirit to live in us. There's only one condition: It's not based on anything we accomplish, but simply faith in God's one and only Son.

Every time we celebrate this supper, it's our job to think through this deal, this covenant God has made with us. As we do, we shift our view from the outward symbol to the inward reality, and in the silence of our hearts we remind God that we're relying on him to carry us through this covenant, to do as he said he would do. That's where God's thoughts meet ours. We exchange glances. He looks at the token (the wine and the bread) and thinks of his promise, while we look at the promise and realize that God is surely going to come through. In the process, we get a clearer, up-close snapshot of our own faith, and faith is the only condition God leaves up to us.

From F. B. Meyer, "The Lord's Supper," a sermon
on Matthew 26:17-29, in *Sermons and Outlines on the
Lord's Supper* (Grand Rapids, MI: Baker, 1951)

Chapter 13

CHRIST AND HIS TABLE COMPANIONS

CHARLES SPURGEON

*C*harles Spurgeon often challenged his congregation to get along or to work together, and his sermons on communion gave him an excellent platform for that kind of exhortation. Here's a short excerpt on one of his powerful calls to Christian unity, from his book Till He Come.

Don't forget there's a pledge of loyalty in the solemn eating and drinking of communion—between the disciples themselves and between the disciples and their Lord. So leave behind all our bickering and jealousy of each other; replace it with an attitude that appreciates other believers and wants the best for them. In fact, if you ever hear anyone bad-mouthing someone you've had communion with, it's your job to stick up for that person. If you hear someone accusing a brother or sister in

Christ, don't just sit there quietly! Another believer's reputation is just as important as yours.

The glue that holds us together should be stronger than anything in any outside club or society. We belong to each other, so let's love each other with intensity and purity. Since we drink the same cup and eat the same bread, let's be sure it's a true symbol of real relationships. As it truly shows how faithful Jesus is to us, let's make sure it truly shows our faithfulness to Jesus—and to each other.

The first disciples trusted their Master and knew he wouldn't lead them down the wrong path. Eating and drinking together was also a way to show how they trusted each other. When Jesus said that one of them would betray him, they didn't suspect each other. Instead, each one asked, "Surely not I, Lord?" (Matthew 26:22). That question shows how much they trusted each other, and Jesus trusted them by treating them as friends. He even trusted them with the great secrets of his coming suffering and death.

How about us? When you gather around the communion table, trust the Lord Jesus totally. If you're suffering, don't doubt his love, but believe that he works all things for your good. If you're loaded down with worry, trust Jesus and leave things in his hands. It won't turn out to be a festival of communion if you come full of suspicion for the Master. Show your trust as you eat with him.

Trust each other, too. Suspicion instantly kills any connection or fellowship you might enjoy. Even if you think another believer has something against you (and it may not even be true), you plant a root of bitterness. Believe in each other! When you meet with others who share communion with you, you might say, "Well, if they deceive me (and unfortunately, they could), then it's better to let it happen than to live life always thinking the worst of fellow Christians."

Why can't Christian fellowship be more real? It ought to mean something. In fact, you have no right to come to that table unless you admit that everyone else who is washed in the blood of Jesus has a claim on your affection. Are you saying you're planning to live with these folks forever in heaven, and yet you don't even like them here on earth? Are you just going to ignore the Master's command to love one another? He gave us all the same badge to wear.

"This is how everyone will recognize that you are my disciples," he said in John 13:35 (MSG). Not by wearing a gold cross or a fish symbol, by the way, but "when they see the love you have for each other."

So that's the Christian's identity card to show we're a disciple of Jesus Christ. Right here, at this communion table, we find fellowship and community. Those who eat this special supper say to the world that they're part of the community of Jesus. A community where we're all pulling the same direction, where we sincerely care about each other, where we're actually members of each other, and members of the body of Christ.

My prayer is that God would make this a reality all over the world, wherever Christians get together. That way, more and more outsiders will be blown away by what they see, and they'll say, "Wow! Look at the way those Christians love each other!"

From Charles Spurgeon, *Till He Come: Communion Meditations and Addresses* (London: Passmore & Alabaster, 1896)

Chapter 14

FOR MANY

ANDREW MURRAY

I t's *fitting that we close out this section with two selections from one of Andrew Murray's finest, but perhaps less appreciated, works. Toward the end of* The Lord's Table, *he gives a heartfelt appeal for Christian unity around the banquet table of Jesus Christ.*

"This is my blood of the covenant, which is poured out for many for the forgiveness of sins" (Matthew 26:28).

Jesus has a big heart. During his last meal on earth, he not only forgot himself to think first of his friends, but in love he looked ahead in time at everyone who would ever be redeemed. He said, "This is my blood of the covenant, which is poured out for many. . . ."

For many . . . By this he told his disciples to build relationships, not just with their buddies at the table, but with the uncounted everyone who would follow Jesus.

For many . . . Around these words we see Jesus breaking

the bread and giving it to his disciples, then again to the crowds after Pentecost (see Acts 2), and yet again to generations of new Christians—an ever-widening circle that includes even us.

The truth of Jesus takes all our puzzling and theological theorizing about the supper and molds them all into one single communion, a single event that includes everyone Jesus has ever touched. It pulls together all these separate circles of Christ-followers into just one church. All our differences and walls disappear in the joyful thought that every believer shares equally in the love and life of the one Head, the one Lord who's passing out the bread. Jesus reaches through calendars, time, and space to draw us right into his presence—just as close as the first disciples who took the bread from Jesus' own hand.

That being the case, the Lord's supper should renew our sense of unity, not only with Christ, but also with his people everywhere. The supper is designed to widen our horizons and enlarge our heart until it's as big as the Lord's. Our love for other believers all over the world should take second place only to our love of the Savior. Remember, he didn't just say this supper is "for you." He also said it was (and is) "for many."

For many . . . For some Christians, it's enough to think of heading up to heaven with their own circle of friends and family. That's not the full picture. Remember, the supper is designed to enlarge our hearts in love and prayer for everyone who belongs to Jesus. We'll know we're where we should be when we're able to rejoice—or weep—with these "strangers" in Christ.

But it doesn't stop there. Real disciples can't help but think of those who are still bogged down in sin, who don't yet know about the blood that was shed "for many." That's because every time we're hit by this true experience—the power of this blood—we get a very real taste of why Jesus went to such great lengths. There's no escape. Those of us who honestly take part in the blood that was shed "for many" lose sight of our own selfishness and self-centered attitudes. In its place our hearts are enlarged to match the heart of Jesus, as we fully embrace the words of our Master: "My blood, shed for many."

Precious Savior, please send me your Spirit, so I'll want the things you want, feel the things you feel, think the things you think. Make me understand how important it is to you that we "make them come in, so that my house will be full" (Luke 14:23). I pray that all your followers will never be able to shake the realization that, just like in the parable of the great feast, "there is still room" (Luke 14:22).

Lord Jesus, you're Love itself. Keep broadcasting that love directly into our hearts through your Holy Spirit. Amen.

From Andrew Murray, *The Lord's Table*
(Grand Rapids, MI: Revell, 1897)

Chapter 15

ONE BODY

ANDREW MURRAY

ere is the second heartfelt appeal from The Lord's Table.

"We, who are many, are one body, for we all partake of the one loaf. . . . A new command I give you: Love one another. As I have loved you, so you must love one another. By this all men will know that you are my disciples, if you love one another" (1 Corinthians 10:17, John 13:34-35).

If we're going to be one with our Lord Jesus, the Head, that means at the same time we're also united with the rest of the body. So when we symbolically eat his body and drink his blood, in the process we're being built right into his body—his entire body. That means not only do we have a relationship with his body that he gave up in death, but also his body that he raised from the dead. What's another word for that kind of raised body?

The church.

It all started when the disciples were knit together in such a new and wonderful way at the Last Supper, the table of the new covenant. The Spirit drew them together with Jesus, as his body, in an entirely new way. That's why the Lord described the kind of love that made it all possible as an entirely new commandment. Remember in John's gospel? "By this all men will know that you are my disciples, if you love one another." The new covenant between God and humans was built on a new life—and also a new love.

We forget this too often at the Lord's table, and it's our great loss as a church. How often have the guests sat at the table of Jesus without knowing or loving each other, without sharing, without caring? Many believers have tried to find a closer relationship with Jesus—but they couldn't, because they would only accept the Head, and not the rest of the body. It's a package deal! But many Christians won't consider the unity of the body, so they miss out on great blessings at the supper.

I wish people would understand: Jesus has to be loved, honored, served, and known . . . *in his body!* In our physical bodies, the blood circulates everywhere and keeps everything connected. So it is with the church. The body of Christ can grow and get stronger only when the Spirit and his love are allowed free access throughout the church, and the life of our Lord can flow from member to member without any barriers.

So when we celebrate this supper, it has to be just as if we're sealing an alliance or a joint venture. One that is not just between the Lord and us, but between the Lord's people—

everyone who comes to the table—and us. Eating together means we're going to live for each other. We want to love and be loved by the Lord at the head of the table, of course. But add to that the love of all those who eat along with us.

> Lord, whom I love, help me to know and to live this truth: As I share fellowship with you through this bread, help me share it with those who also eat this bread with me. As I receive you, so I receive them. As I want to love and serve you, to belong to you, help me to love and serve them, too. In Christ we belong to each other. I humbly confess to you the sins of my old nature: selfishness, a lack of love, envy, a bad temper, a "who cares?" attitude, so much more. I trust you now for your love, gentleness, and mercy, so that I can spread these gifts to others. O Jesus, as you give yourself to me, please work in me and with me. Please spread your love to all who share this one loaf with me. Amen.

> From Andrew Murray, *The Lord's Table*
> (Grand Rapids, MI: Revell, 1897)

PUTTING THE WORDS
TO WORK

QUESTIONS FOR INDIVIDUAL
OR GROUP STUDY

Use these questions as springboards for individual or group study.

1. Imagine that you were to read Andrew Murray's "The Divine Invitation" aloud to the congregation at the beginning of your next communion service. How do you think people would react? What would they say? How do you think the words would make them feel? And then how would you feel? List several adjectives to describe your reaction.

2. In "The Lord's Supper," F. B. Meyer listed several different words, different ways to look at the Lord's Supper. On a piece of paper, list each word and its short definition. Which word best describes the way you look at the ceremony? Have you ever looked at it any other way?

3. Have you ever thought about Meyer's point that when we share the Lord's supper, we're declaring our fellowship with the rest of Christ's body? What are some practical ways you can experience that reality? What are some ways you can share that idea with others?

4. Meyer says that during communion we "exchange glances" with God. How do you do that?

5. Meyer describes communion as a covenant, while Charles Spurgeon describes it as a pledge of loyalty. Do you see any differences between those two ideas, or are they the same? Explain your opinion.

6. In "Christ and His Table Companions," Spurgeon talks about how important it is to build up our love for each other as a witness to the world. What does that idea have to do with the Lord's supper? If you were to follow Spurgeon's advice, what would change in your life?

7. In "For Many" Murray reminds us of the bigger picture, the larger church. What are some ways you can keep from focusing too much on just you and your local church?

8. In his prayer ("For Many"), Murray asks that God would help him "want the things you want, feel the things you feel, think the things you think." What's the key to success in this request?

9. According to Murray in "One Body," what keeps some Christians from experiencing a closer relationship with Jesus?

10. Look at some of the sins Murray names, and add your

own. How do they relate to communion? Use your list in your own private prayer time, before your next time of communion.

PART TWO

GRACE
TO HEAL

RECONCILIATION

THROUGHOUT THE AGES, RECONCILIATION has been one of the central graces of the church. This is probably because the central work of history has been one of reconciliation: Jesus reconciling all people to God through his work on the cross. What Christian doesn't understand how Jesus bridged the gap caused by our sin?

What's not so obvious is how we as Christians can put feet on this truth, how we are to live out in our lives what we understand in our heads and have accepted in our hearts. In other words, what difference does it make in our everyday lives to be forgiven by the Creator of the universe? How do we respond to so great a love? Will it make a difference in the way we make decisions, in the time we spend, in the investments we make? What's more, will forgiveness from God flavor our own personal relationships? Will the fact that we're forgiven make any difference in the way we speak to a person on the street, a waitress, or our mail carrier?

It can, and it must. Problem is, the evangelical church we love so much does well with some aspects of forgiveness, perhaps not so well with others. For instance, we might com-partmentalize God's forgiveness, paint it into a corner, and tell it, "This far and no further." Forgiveness is welcomed in the evangelistic sermon. Forgiveness is front and center when Billy Graham gives the altar call. And so it should be.

After the service, however, we may grapple with the prac-tical aspects of forgiveness, especially those aspects that have any resemblance to forgiveness and reconciliation as practiced in Christian traditions not our own. But is it possible that we are missing something rich and useful to the life of our church? To find out, we stop for a moment to consider what the early reformers had to say about the subject. Martin Luther, for example, the parish priest, had a few questions for church leadership. Or we listen to the teaching of Andrew Murray. Yes, they spoke to different audiences, but what if their words still have something to tell us . . . even today? What if the truth of their interpretations of Scripture continues to echo over the centuries, calling us to reexamine our faith and practice? It's a question worth asking. So let's take a step back and listen, always keeping in mind the example of the Jews in Berea, a city in what is now northeastern Greece. The Bible records that Jews there "received Paul's message with enthusiasm and met with him daily, examining the Scriptures to see if they supported what he said" (Acts 17:11, MSG).

Good for them. And good for us, if we do the same thing. Then, if we see anything lacking in our own faith—or in the practice of our own fellowship—may God grant us the courage to knit these truths back into the fabric of our walk with him.

Chapter 16

CONFESSION 101

ANDREW MURRAY

Back in the late 1800s, Andrew Murray had a heart for seeing young people get right with God. Interesting how the advice he gave students in 1891 was on the mark then, and even more so today. In this chapter from his book The New Life, Murray gets right down to the basics by explaining what confession really is, how we can do it, and why it matters.

"If we admit our sins . . . he won't let us down; he'll be true to himself. He'll forgive our sins and purge us of all wrongdoing" (1 John 1:9, MSG).

God hates one thing. It makes him sick, makes him steaming mad, and in the end, he will wipe it out.

It's sin. Living life away from God's standards.

So what's the one thing that makes people unhappy? Sin.

The one thing that Jesus gave his blood for? Sin.

The one thing we all have to bring to God before we can

have anything to do with him or talk with him? Sin.

You understood this—at least to some degree—when you first came to Jesus. Now it's time to dig deeper. My best advice is to bring your sin to the One who can take it each day, to the only One who can take it away, God himself. Understand that one of the biggest perks of being a Christian is being able to confess your sin to the Lord, unloading the guilt.

Only God's holiness—his all-powerful sinlessness—can pulverize our sins, and here's how: By confession we hand them over to God, and he tosses them into his blast oven where holy love consumes them. The bottom line is that God—and only God—takes away our sins.

Problem is, Christians don't always get this. We want to paint over sin, or to pretend that what we've done isn't all that bad. We'll face up to it only in emergencies, like just before we want to make a good impression with the Lord.

Or we think getting rid of sin is a do-it-yourself project, as if feeling sorry for ourselves can sweeten it up. Or maybe we can make it all better by just straightening up our act.

No way. If we want to be right with God and if we're looking for the lighthearted happiness that comes with it, confession is the only way. True confession is God's gift to us; it's one of the deepest roots of a spiritual life—a life that's filled with power to do the right thing.

So when you lay out your sin to God, get specific. Fuzzy-talk such as, "I'm sorry if I did something wrong," does more harm than good, and it's better to tell God, "I don't have anything specific to confess yet."

Start small. Bring just one thing to God that you know you've done wrong, and before you go on, get completely right with him about it. Be clear that this one sin is now in God's hands. Confession will lead you to a place where you can start to grow and make real changes. God offers power and blessing through confession.

Be straight with God. Don't forget that in confession you're delivering up your sin so it can be disposed of—and when you do this, you need to believe that God is in the business of sin disposal.

You also need to be ready to let your sin go, so that you don't repeat the same sin over and over again. So by confessing you're saying "no more!" Don't confess if you're not sick and tired of the sin, if you're not ready to turn your back on it for good, if you don't want God to set you free of its clutches. Confession is good only for a full transfer, giving up all that sin to God.

When you confess, trust. Believe that God will do what he says he's going to do, which is clean you up. Then don't stop confessing, keep shoveling the junk of your life (your sin) into God's holy bonfire until your soul is good with the fact that God has taken care of the problem. This kind of faith will take you past the world's booby traps and will help you leave sin in the dust. Starting from this kind of faith, God in Jesus will truly set you free from sin.

Remember, though, that four things can mess up the process. One, not understanding the concept of what sin is, and how it keeps us from knowing God better. Two, understanding, but being afraid to bother an awesome God with our dirty little secrets. (We shouldn't be afraid.) Three, trying to fix it ourselves by putting a nice spin on things we've done wrong. (It never works.) And four, not believing that Jesus has the power to dropkick our sin and take us to a better place in life, snapping the chains of sin. (He can, and he will.)

But what if you lie to someone, or catch yourself doing something else you know is wrong? Should you confess it right out to God, or wait for later, when things settle down? No question there: Confess it now. Don't wait another minute. Bring everything to God on the spot, and don't water it down.

By the way, confession isn't always just to God. If you've done something against a person (and that's usually the case), it's also worthwhile to confess to that person. Sure, it may be harder to confess to a person than just to God. But the Bible says to each of us, "Confess your sins to each other and pray for each other so that you can live together whole and healed" (James 5:16, MSG).

So, fellow believer, do you get it now? Here's a quiz.

Q: What do you do with sin in your life? Every sin?

A: Confess it to God. Give it to God. He's the only one who can take it out of your life.

Lord God, how can I thank you for this incredible blessing, being able to come to you when I've blown it? You know how sin and your holiness don't mix. You know I'd rather pretend that I never sin, or try to come to you looking better than I really am. So please teach me to just come to you with my sin—every sin. Teach me how to confess my sin, to lay it down, and give it all to you. Amen.

From Andrew Murray, "The Confession of Sin," in
The New Life: Words of God for Young Disciples of Christ
(New York: Hurst & Co., 1891)

Chapter 17

DOES EVERYONE ELSE HAVE TO KNOW?

MARTIN LUTHER

Early church reformer Martin Luther had a lot to say about confessing sins. That's no surprise, since he was part of a movement in the early 1500s that took the Bible as its bottom line—rather than church tradition or the opinions of church leaders. But what about things such as "private" confession, where people would regularly come to a priest and tell him their sins . . . in private? Let's take a look at some of what he wrote to see if it still makes sense today.

I wouldn't let anybody take private confession away from me. In fact, I wouldn't give it up for anything, because I know this kind of confession has given me comfort and strength. People who struggle and fight with the Devil know what confession can do for them, too. If not for confession, the Devil would have taken me out a long time ago. That's because we can't handle all those daily doubts and troubles by ourselves, so we take a friend aside and share our heart. How can it hurt to humble yourself in front of a friend? A little shame isn't such a bad thing. Because when the other Christian offers you a boost, take that comforting word as if you heard it from God himself.

From Martin Luther's sermon in Wittenberg,
Germany (March 16, 1522)

Even though we can't trace our church custom of private confession straight to a command in the Bible, I still like it. It helps to confess our sins to each other. I'd even say it's *needed* in the church, and we shouldn't get rid of it as the church changes. In fact, I'm glad we still do it this way in our churches, because private confession is strong medicine for when we're hit hard by sin.

From Martin Luther, *The Babylonian Captivity of the Church* (1520)

We should hang on to private confession in the church. That's because when sin does a number on our consciences, private confession helps even more than hearing a public sermon could. We want to open the door of confession as if it were a refuge, a retreat from the hopeless feeling of being trapped and worn down by the Devil. There's nothing worse than not having someone who can give you friendly advice and a sympathetic ear. So let's keep the door open to people who need support from a pastor. Or if the sin is so deep that the person can't share with a minister, they can share with another believer, a strong

Christian, and ask for advice. That way, if people hear God's Word about how their sins can be washed away, whether it's from a pastor or from someone else, they'll be spiritually and emotionally lifted up. Even if they were beaten up by the Devil and the ill effects of their mistakes, they'll be healed.

From Martin Luther's lectures on Genesis 36:20-30 (1536)

Sincere confession isn't a matter of reciting a long list of preprinted prayers during a worship service. The main ingredient of true confession is a burning desire to get right with God. Here's all it takes: telling God you are guilty, and confessing to him that you are a sinner. We shouldn't ask anything else of people, and we shouldn't require them to name and recite all their infractions publicly—unless they truly want to, or if something specific is really bothering them, and they need specific advice and comfort about it.

From Martin Luther's Easter sermon (1531)

Chapter 18

LIKE CHRIST: IN FORGIVING

ANDREW MURRAY

No one had more to say about life together as Christians than the popular South African pastor, Andrew Murray. In his book Like Christ, Murray explores what it means to live in a radical new way—the way the Master would have us live, beyond just feeling forgiven. In this chapter he tackles the deeper issue of how to pass along God's forgiveness.

"Be even-tempered, content with second place, quick to forgive an offense. Forgive as quickly and completely as the Master forgave you" (Colossians 3:13, MSG).

When we're living a grace-filled life, one of the first blessings God gives us is forgiveness. It's also one of the most awesome of blessings. Through forgiveness we change lanes, change direction from an old life to the new road. Forgiveness is a sign from God that he promises to love us, no matter what. It's also the open door through which God showers us with all his spiritual gifts.

What's more, there's absolutely no way the people who are bought with God's love can ever forget they're forgiven sinners. Not in a million years, not here, and not even in heaven. That's because nothing sets our love for God on fire more than the experience of knowing God's forgiving love. Nothing builds up our courage more. God's Holy Spirit makes sure we don't forget it. Every day, every time we think on the Lord, every thought reminds us that we owe everything to the forgiveness we never deserved.

This forgiving love is one of the most awesome ingredients of a life that's filled and fueled by God. It's the ingredient that best shows everyone how God is behind all this life-building. It gives believers the best chance to tell him "Thank you!" or "Praise you!"

But it doesn't stop there. As soon as we recognize all the forgiveness that he's poured into our own lives, he wants us to pass it all right along to others.

Ever notice how often Jesus talked about this brand of "pass it on" forgiveness? When we check out what he said in Matthew 6:12 and 18:21-35, as well as in Mark 11:25, we can't miss how the two parts of forgiveness are braided together: As God forgives us, we have to forgive others.

Paul said the same thing in his letter to the Colossians: "Forgive as quickly and completely as the Master forgave you." So we have to copy God, we have to copy Jesus, in forgiving.

It's not hard to figure out why. God doesn't shower his forgiving love on us to save us from punishment. There's much more to it than that. Forgiving love wins us over, makes us God's property, lives in us. It puts God's stamp on us. Forgiving love doesn't lose its heavenly flavor, either. It still needs to do its thing—not just for us, but through us, showing us the way and giving us the power to forgive others.

Forgiving love doesn't stop with me. That's so true, that the Bible even says that not forgiving others is a sure sign we didn't accept God's forgiving love in the first place. If we only want to grab the part of forgiveness that will keep us out of trouble—and not the full measure of God's forgiveness that comes in to rule our heart and life—well, that proves we've not accepted 100 percent of God's forgiving love.

On the other hand, if we do say "yes!" to the whole measure of God's forgiveness, the joy that we experience as we forgive others is ongoing proof of the reality of God's forgiving love in us. We receive forgiving love *from Jesus,* and pass it along to others, *like Jesus.*

These two are one.

Obviously the Bible and the church teach all this. Fine, but what do the lives and experience of Christians tell us? This is where the problem comes in. First, a lot of believers hardly know what the Bible teaches about the depth of God's forgiving love and what it can do in our lives. Or, if they have read about it in the Bible, they have a hard time believing we're up to it. Even if they do agree, they find all kinds of excuses to not plug the truth into their lives. Even Christian leaders manage to say things like, "Well, they'd never forgive me if the shoe were on the other foot!" All these excuses are from the pit.

Look how simple was the command of Jesus—and its flip side: "You can't get forgiveness from God . . . without also forgiving others."

Our excuses can shut down the power of God's Word in our lives, and who wants that?

Through forgiving love, God gives us power to overcome the world's evil. Remember when Jesus said we should forgive seventy times seven times?

Through forgiving love, we model our lives on what Jesus has done—not on what a person might do to us.

This is the sign that we've opened the door to God's forgiveness in our own lives: We don't follow the example of other people—not even people we think are ideal Christians. We simply follow Jesus.

I wish it weren't true, but so many people in so many churches don't follow the law of forgiving love. Not at home or in everyday life. Not even in missions projects or at church. Christians just don't seem to hear and follow the call of Jesus to forgive . . . just as he forgave.

We disagree with someone, or someone else tries to stop our great idea. A person disrespects us, or we hear someone talking us down. So we resent it, we fight back, or we don't have anything to do with that individual. What? The law of compassion, love, and forgiveness has yet to take root here. We should instead be loving, forgiving, and forgetting, *just like Jesus*. That's how the body of Christ is supposed to work.

Dear Christian brothers and sisters, we're called to be like Jesus for the rest of the world to see. That means we need to remember something basic: Since forgiving your sins was one of the first things Jesus did for you, then forgiving others should be one of the first things we do *for him*.

Don't forget also that even if it feels sweet to be forgiven, it's going to feel even sweeter when we pass along that same forgiveness to others. That's because the joy of being forgiven is ours in the here and now. That's great, as far as it goes. But we can live in a bigger joy when we forgive others, because that joy belongs to Jesus and it's flavored by the place it comes from: heaven.

You've got to understand! We share in the work of Jesus when we pass along forgiveness. He calls us to soak up the same joy he himself experiences! How amazing is that?

This is how we can bless the world, following the blueprint of Jesus. After all, Jesus both overcomes his enemies and makes lifetime friends . . . as the forgiving One. As the forgiving One, he builds and expands his kingdom, his family. Only his forgiving love can win the world over—not just in what we say, but also lived out in the lives of those who follow him. After all, if people see us loving and forgiving as Jesus did, they'll have no choice but to admit that God is real and that he is here.

If this all seems too far out of reach, or even impossible, remember that's only true if we're trying to force it, make it happen on our own. Our original sin nature just isn't compatible with (and can't produce) the joy God wants to give us.

But! Join forces with Jesus and make it so. Because when

we lean on him, he takes us in his stride. If you tell Jesus, "I surrender all of me," then he custom-fits his Holy Spirit to take you along for the ride, as well. Even before you hit the rough waters of temptation—a riptide that would pull you under—practice watching Jesus, keeping your eyes only on him. His beautiful, forgiving love is your best example, the best place to start. As the apostle Paul told the Corinthian believers, "Our lives gradually [become] brighter and more beautiful as God enters our lives and we become like him" (2 Corinthians 3:17-19, MSG).

So every time you pray or thank God you're forgiven, promise also that you'll show the same forgiving love to people you meet. But before you even get to the point of having to forgive others, open your heart to be filled with love for Jesus, for other Christians, even for people you don't know or don't care for.

After all, a love-filled heart is primed and then blessed even more when it in turn forgives. Let go each time you're tempted to hoard your share of forgiveness. In so doing, you'll prove you live in the center of God's forgiving love. You'll see how good it is to refocus God's forgiving light on to others. And you'll experience the privilege and blessing of being stamped in the image of the Lord you love.

From Andrew Murray, *Like Christ*
(Grand Rapids, MI: Revell, 1895)

PUTTING THE WORDS TO WORK

QUESTIONS FOR INDIVIDUAL OR GROUP STUDY

Use these questions as springboards for individual or group study.

1. In "Confession 101" Andrew Murray speculates a little about God's anger. Based on what you know about God, how would you describe God's emotions? What makes God angry, and why?

2. List some of the ways Murray says Christians try to deal with sin. What are the results?

3. What keeps you from confession?

4. On separate paper, write down Murray's five steps to confession. (Get specific. Start small. Be straight. Let it go. Trust.) Then write your own definitions for these steps.

5. In "Does Everyone Else Have to Know?" Martin Luther seems to favor the custom of confessing to each other, or

"private confession." Explain his reasons. Could any of them apply to our church today?

6. According to Luther, why is private confession not just for paid professional clergy?

7. Think about what your church would be like if everyone agreed with Luther and private confession were a normal part of church life. What do you think would be the results?

8. In "Like Christ" Andrew Murray says that we'll never forget we're forgiven sinners, not even in heaven. Do you agree? What do you think it would be like in heaven to remember your sins, as well as the grace that brought you forgiveness?

9. Murray refers to a special kind of forgiveness described in Matthew 6:12 and 18:21-35, as well as Mark 11:25. What does it take to realize this kind of forgiveness? What happens if we don't?

10. Describe in your own words the twofold aspect of forgiveness Murray is talking about in "Like Christ." Is it possible to have one part of that forgiveness without the other? How would that kind of forgiveness work in your life?

PRAYER FOR THE SICK AND HURTING

EACH GENERATION MUST REDISCOVER the deepest truths of Scripture for themselves. Sometimes the truth is buried, often it just needs a little dusting off. Other times it's been distorted or taken to places it should never be.

So it is with prayer for the sick, which down through the years has been counted a privilege for believers in Christ. Yet here is a gift from God that because of its nature has been twisted into the constrictions of the freak show and the Vegas magic act. Poof! Smoke and mirrors tell us the woman has been sawn in half, and yet . . .

This is not the healing of Jesus, the healing of the disciples, the healing that Scripture instructs us to take part in or pray for. What happened, and what's missing? Healing—or the lack of it—seems to be part of a larger picture, a deeper discovery to be made of a God who has plans we don't always understand.

So we look back to the writings of anointed followers of

Jesus, and naturally back to Scripture itself, to seek a better picture. Here perhaps the smoke begins to clear as we see beyond the fanfare to the genuine article and the God who heals.

For he does heal, and yet we still might wonder . . . how, and when? Is there a pattern we must follow? Certain errors or denominational trapdoors we must avoid? We'll let the writers in this section lead the way as we explore these issues for ourselves, and then we'll see if any of the answers might not apply to our churches today.

Or whether they surprise us.

Chapter 19

ON VISITING THE SICK

JOHN WESLEY

Although John Wesley is best known for his tireless preaching and evangelism throughout the 1700s, he also was vitally concerned with health issues. In this sermon excerpt, he begins with our Lord's command to care for the sick, then asks "Does it apply to me?" The answer is a clear "yes," no matter what our station in life. Here's some practical advice from Pastor Wesley.

"I was sick and you stopped to visit" (Matthew 25:36, MSG).

For right now, let's just look at one thing: visiting the sick. It's something everyone who's well should do, one way or another. But even those of us who say we love the Lord don't do it enough. So I have to ask, who should be visiting the sick?

People who are rich in this world have a special calling from God to this work. After all, they have more time and resources at hand. But how about those who aren't as well off? Should they worry about it? After all, if a low-income person can hardly put bread on the table, what can that individual share with others? Well, just because you don't have everything, doesn't mean you also need to be cut out of the blessings you get from looking out for others. Even someone who's not rich can spot the truth in the saying: "Let our conveniences give way to our neighbor's necessities, and our necessities give way to our neighbor's extreme needs."

Not many folks are so poor that they can't spare what the King James Version calls "two mites." Remember the story of the widow in Mark 12, who was praised by Jesus for giving all that she had? Even so, if you don't have any funds to spare, you can still pass along something that's more valuable. Yes, you do have something that's worth much more than a millionaire's stock portfolio!

That's right. Peter told the lame beggar that he didn't have any cash on hand, but he had something better from his Lord. He had healing! In the same way, if you speak in the name of Jesus of Nazareth—just like Peter did—your words are health to the soul. They're comfort to the body. You say you don't have anything? No way. By passing along God's grace (of which you have plenty!) you offer more than all the world is worth.

So go on, even if you don't have deep pockets. Just follow the pattern Jesus set while he was here on the earth. Whenever you get a chance, make a difference for the Lord. Bring healing to people whose lives are weighed down by the Devil. Show them how to shake off their chains and fly to Jesus! He's the One who sets the prisoners free, and who breaks the shackles from their necks.

But above all, give them your prayers. Pray with them. Pray for them. And who knows? You might see them saved, as well!

From John Wesley, "On Visiting the Sick," sermon originally preached in 1786 when he was in his early eighties

Chapter 20

THE INVITATION

SØREN KIERKEGAARD

Danish philosopher Søren Kierkegaard is studied on college campuses around the world. For those of us who don't dabble much in mind-bending philosophies, much of his writing seems out of reach. Even so, there's an element of Christ-centered simplicity in much of his thought, as in this piece, "The Invitation." After all, this is the man who wrote in his journal, "I never forget how God helps me and it is therefore my last wish that everything may be to his honor" (Journals, November 20, 1847).

Jesus said, "I will give you rest." Isn't it strange? We have to understand his "come to me" invitation from Matthew 11:28 to mean "Stay with me; I am rest." How very different this is from so many well-intentioned people who say "Come on in" but who then say "Our time is up. See you later." This is not like a person who gives us a referral, tells us where to find help, or who suggests a useful treatment they've heard of.

Not at all. This helper opens his arms and invites every one of us—everyone who's bruised, exhausted, or beaten down—to come to him. He promises to fold us into his heart, as he tells us, "Stay with me now, because staying with me *is* rest." So the Helper himself is the help!

Yes, it's strange. But the God who invites everyone to himself and who wants to help us all has a custom-made plan for every sick person. It's as if everyone who comes to God with an illness is his only patient!

Compare that to a regular doctor, who divides his time among all his patients. Even if he has a huge patient list, it's nothing like the Lord's. So each doctor does his exam, writes out a prescription, and tells us what to do . . . and then hurries off to another patient. He obviously can't allow us to hang around with him in his home or office all day, and he certainly can't sit with one patient too long while ignoring all his other patients. So it's clear that the helper and the help are two different things. As patients we cling to whatever help or treatment we receive all day, but we're able to see the doctor only once in a while.

On the other hand, if the helper is also the help, then he will remain with the patient all day and all night. Isn't it strange that this is just the kind of helper who invites us all to himself?

From Søren Kierkegaard, *Preparation for a Christian Life,*
from *Selections from the Writings of Søren Kierkegaard,* trans.
L. M. Hollander (Austin, TX: University of Texas, 1923)

Chapter 21

THE MORE
EXCELLENT WAY

JOHN WESLEY

As a pastor and church leader, John Wesley worked hard to bring Christians together. He is known as the founder of Methodism, and for his famous sermon "The More Excellent Way," which is based on Paul's words to the Corinthian Christians as recorded in 1 Corinthians 12:31. Here's a small part of that sermon.

"Eagerly desire the greater gifts. And now I will show you the most excellent way" (1 Corinthians 12:31).

In the verses leading up to this passage, the apostle Paul had been discussing the extraordinary gifts of the Holy Spirit—things such as healing the sick, prophesy, speaking in languages the speaker has never learned, and interpreting these languages. Paul said it's good to want these gifts. In fact, he encouraged Corinthian Christians to pursue them. That way, the believers might become better equipped to serve both the church and those still outside the church. Then Paul says, "Now I will show you the most excellent way."

This way [love] is head and shoulders above all the rest put together, since it will always lead us to happiness both in this world and in the world to come. Even if you were filled with all those other special gifts like no one else, you could still be miserable now and for all time.

From John Wesley, "The More Excellent Way,"
a sermon delivered in 1787

Chapter 22

PREVAILING PRAYER: WHAT HINDERS IT?

D. L. MOODY

When Dwight L. (D. L.) Moody spoke to his congregation, he peppered his messages with true-life examples, common people who exemplified his points. Perhaps that was the appeal of one of America's most successful evangelists—his common touch. Like Billy Graham several generations later, Moody knew what ordinary people were thinking, since he was one himself! Even so, his messages were far from ordinary. Here he talks about submitting to God's will, and how it fits right in with praying for healing. It's an excerpt from his book about Prevailing Prayer.

Real prayer is when I'm raised up with God, when I know I'm joined with God and his purposes. Real prayer is when I step fully into God's will and carry out his purpose totally. Sometimes I'm afraid we get prayer completely turned around, as if we can talk God into doing whatever pops into our minds, or whatever would help us reach our foolish, weak-sighted goals.

It's not that way at all. I'm convinced that God knows what is best for me and for the rest of the world, much better than I ever could. Even if I were granted the power to say, "My will be done," I would rather say to him, "Your will be done."

I heard of a gravely sick woman who was asked if she was willing to live . . . or die.

"Whatever God pleases," she answered.

"Yes, but if God left the final decision up to you," came the question, "which would you choose?"

"I'm telling you," she came back, "I would turn it right back over to God."

So there's a perfect example of how a person's choice can be folded into God's. She who received her will from God is the one who first subjected her will to God.

Even so, it's not always an easy thing to offer our hearts completely up to God's will and God's way. So perhaps we should adopt this version of the prayer that has been attributed to French bishop Francois Fenelon:

> O God, take my heart for I cannot give it; and when
> you have it, keep it—for I cannot keep it for you.
> Save me in spite of myself.

Some of the world's spiritual giants have struggled with this challenge. Moses could pray for Israel, and God listened to him. But God didn't answer some of Moses' smallest personal prayers. He asked that God would let him cross the Jordan and that he might see Lebanon in Canaan. After wandering forty years in the desert, he wanted to step into the promised land.

But the Lord said "no."

Was that a sign that God didn't love Moses? Of course not. God loved him greatly. Yet God did not answer Moses' prayer.

Sometimes your child might say, "I want it!" But you don't always answer the request, since you know it can't be good for children to get everything they want, just like that. Moses wanted to enter the promised land, but the Lord had something else planned for him. As someone once said, "God kissed away his soul, and took him home to himself." God buried Moses, the greatest honor ever paid a man.

Fifteen hundred years later God did answer Moses' prayer. He allowed him to go into the promised land and get a glimpse of the coming glory. You remember that Moses was on the mount of transfiguration, with Elijah, Peter, James, and John. He heard a voice from God's throne: "This is my Son, marked by my love, focus of my delight. Listen to him" (Matthew 17:5, MSG).

For Moses, this was better than being able to cross the Jordan, the way Joshua did, and live thirty years in the land of Canaan. So when our prayers for things here on earth are not answered, let's submit to God's will, and know that it's all right.

I've heard of a deaf and mute boy who was once asked why he thought he was born handicapped. He wrote his answer on a chalkboard, quoting our Lord Jesus: "Yes, Father, for this was your good pleasure" (Matthew 11:26).

Of course Elijah was mighty in prayer. He brought fire from heaven down on his sacrifice, and rain down on a thirsty land. He stood without fear before King Ahab in the power of prayer. Yet we find him sitting under a juniper tree like a coward, begging God to let him die. (See 1 Kings 19:4.)

No, the Lord loved Elijah too well for that. God ended up taking him up to heaven in a chariot of fire.

So we can't allow the Devil to take advantage of us, making us believe God doesn't love us just because he doesn't answer all our prayers exactly when, where, and how we want him to.

Moses takes up more room in the Old Testament than anyone else; it's the same with Paul in the New Testament (except the Lord himself). Yet Paul didn't know how to pray for himself! He begged the Lord to take away his "thorn in the flesh." God didn't answer that prayer directly, but gave Paul a greater blessing. He gave him more grace. (See 2 Corinthians 12:7-9.)

So maybe we have some trial, some thorn in the flesh. If God doesn't choose to take it away, let's ask him to give us more grace, grace to bear it.

We read that Paul found something to celebrate even when things went wrong and he suffered physical problems—because he realized God power's rested on him all the more. May God in his grace help us to say with Paul, "In all things God works for the good of those who love him" (Romans 8:28). So when we pray to God, we need to submit and say, "Your will be done."

In John's gospel account we read that "if you . . . ." (That "if" is a mountain to begin with!) "If you remain in me and my words remain in you, ask whatever you wish, and it will be given you" (15:7).

People quote the last half of this verse often, but not the first half. There's not a whole lot of remaining in Jesus these days. We go and visit him once in a while, and that's it. But here's the key: If Jesus is in my heart, of course I'm not going to ask anything that is against his will.

How many of us have God's Words remaining in us? We need to ask ourselves why we're praying a particular way. If we really want something, we should search Scripture to see if we have a right to ask it. Because there are plenty of things we want that aren't good for us, while many of the things we'd go out of our way to avoid are really our best blessings.

A friend of mine was shaving one morning when his little boy, not four years old, asked him for his razor. The little guy wanted to whittle a piece of wood with it. When he couldn't have the razor, he started to wail as if his heart would break.

You see the analogy. I'm afraid too many of us are praying for razors. John Bunyan, who wrote *Pilgrim's Progress* while in jail for preaching the gospel, blessed God for that jail more than anything else that happened to him. While we never pray for tough times, they're often the best thing we could ask for.

From D. L. Moody, *Prevailing Prayer: What Hinders It?*
(Grand Rapids, MI: Revell, 1884)

Chapter 23

THE GOSPEL OF HEALING

A. B. SIMPSON

Canadian-born evangelist Albert (A. B.) Simpson is well-known for his work among the poor and immigrants in nineteenth century New York. He's also known for his work in Christian publishing, writing books and hymns, founding the Christian & Missionary Alliance — and a deep faith in God for healing. How does healing work? What does it take? Are there limits? Though Simpson wrote much on the subject, here's just a portion from one of his books.

Healing is not the immortal life. How do people die, if Christ always heals? The thing is that faith goes only as far as God's promise, and God has never promised we're not going to die in this life. The promise? A full life, strength and health up to the limits of this natural life, until our life work is done.

Yes, the Bible says we're living a resurrection life. But this isn't the whole deal, just the "firstfruits." A taste. God describes our immortal life in Scripture, where Paul says that "it is God who has made us for this very purpose and has given us the Spirit as a deposit, guaranteeing what is to come" (2 Corinthians 5:5).

In other words, this deposit is a handful of the soil from this farm Jesus bought. But only a handful. So through his Holy Spirit, God has given us a new physical life, a handful of resurrection life. But again it's only a handful, and the fullness won't come until his Second Coming. Ah, but that handful is worth all our natural lives and all the soil of earth, a hundred times over.

From A. B. Simpson, *The Gospel of Healing*
(Camp Hill, PA: Christian Publications, 1915)

Chapter 24

OF EXTREME UNCTION

JOHN CALVIN

I n his The Institutes of the Christian Religion, *John Calvin presents a spirited defense of his faith, often in response to what he felt were historic misinterpretations of Scripture. In this section he tackles the practice of "extreme unction," or healing ceremonies for the gravely ill, by contrasting his era's practices with biblical standards. Here's a portion of his argument, under the heading "Of Extreme Unction, So Called."*

Read in the Gospels how the disciples of Jesus obeyed the command of their Lord on their first solo mission. It says that "right and left they sent the demons packing; they brought wellness to the sick, anointing their bodies, healing their spirits" (Mark 6:13, MSG). As they healed, they used oil. James mentions this when he orders church leaders to anoint the sick. But really, there's plainly nothing magic, and there's no deep mystery behind anointing with oil. Just look at the flexibility both Jesus and his disciples have in this matter.

For example, when Jesus was about to give sight to a blind man, he used a little lump of clay that he made by spitting on the ground. He healed some people as he touched them, others just by saying the word. In the same way, the disciples cured some diseases just by a word, some by touching the sick person, and still others by anointing with oil.

I don't think any of these methods were random. I also don't think the methods in themselves had anything to do with the cure itself. They were just symbols to remind ordinary people (people who didn't always get it) that healing comes 100 percent from God. The methods used were just tools to keep us from giving credit to people, to the disciples.

Now, there's no doubt that the Lord is present with his people back then, and now, and in all ages. He cures our sicknesses as much as we need him to—and no less than he ever did. But he doesn't dispense miracles through the disciples any more. That was a temporary gift.

From John Calvin, *The Institutes of the Christian Religion,* "Of Extreme Unction, So Called" (1559), trans. Henry Beveridge, *Calvin's Institutes* (Grand Rapids, MI: Christian Classics Ethereal Library, 1845)

Chapter 25

HE KEPT SAYING . . .

A. B. SIMPSON

Reverend A. B. Simpson speculated about Paul's "thorn in the flesh," though he, like so many others, really couldn't be sure what it was. Even so, he had interesting ideas about it and how it related to prayer. Here's an excerpt from another of his books on the role of divine healing in the life of the church.

"He said to me, 'My grace is sufficient for you'" (2 Corinthians 12:9).

It's a good thing we don't know exactly what Paul's "thorn in the flesh" really was. Because now any one of us can put ourselves in Paul's shoes, and enjoy the comfort of imagining that our problem was Paul's too.

Whatever the "thorn" was, though, we know one thing for sure: It didn't keep Paul from serving, all out.

So if you want to apply Paul's tough times to being disabled, good luck. For sure Paul wasn't disabled by it. Just read in the next paragraph of 2 Corinthians 12, where Paul says that "the things that mark an apostle—signs, wonders and miracles—were done among you . . . " (12:12). In the same chapter he says that God gave him more strength and power with the thorn than without it. So Paul was happy the way he was, gave God all the credit. He found that when he himself was weak, then God made him stronger.

Here's where we find an important prayer lesson. How often should we pray for a thing? Paul prayed three times about his thorn. Actually, he prayed until God assured him of his answer.

Probably this is the best lesson on prayer we can learn: Pray about something until we understand God's mind about it. Pray until we get enough light, direction, and comfort. Pray until our hearts are quieted and satisfied.

It's good to remember that there is a difference between babbling at God, and keeping on in persistent prayer. God's Spirit is going to guide in each case, but a heaven-taught heart will pray until it can't pray any more. We should shift our praying to praise as soon as the okay from God arrives.

Sometimes that assurance arrives instantly—other times it takes asking, seeking, and knocking on God's door. That's supplication.

And Paul's answer to prayer? God didn't take away the thorn, as Paul had asked. Instead, God substituted something far better—strength that empowered Paul far more than he would normally expect, so he could do more than if God had "fixed" the problem the way Paul had wanted.

There are two ways to solve a problem: Simply remove it,

or double your strength to deal with it. For example, if you're in a battle, the enemy might retreat and allow you to march to triumph. Or your commander might send double reinforcements. Either way, you win.

Or if you're trying to make your way up a river with a dangerously rocky bottom, you might avoid running your boat aground in one of two ways: by deepening the channel or by raising the water level.

That's what God did for Paul. He deepened the river and lifted Paul above the rocks in his life, making him (as it says in Romans 8:37) more than a conqueror.

Here's the application. Sometimes in our spiritual life, the Lord allows even our thoughts and feelings to grow into irritating and painful thorns.

What to do? Just lean more on Jesus as we press through the pain. We can ignore the worst thoughts and feelings as we trust and believe in him. In Jesus we can stand firm and win over any enemy. As we look back on these hurdles, we see that winning with Jesus is a much higher high, a much sweeter sweet.

Sometimes in our physical life, when we accept the Lord's help for healing, the physical pain or problem remains—he doesn't take it right away. But to compensate, God will give us an amazing shot of energy and strength so that we move beyond the pain and go on with the work he has for us—thorn or no thorn.

From A. B. Simpson, *Friday Meeting Talks* (New York: Christian Alliance Publishing Co., 1894)

PUTTING THE WORDS TO WORK

Use these questions as springboards for individual or group study.

1. According to John Wesley, in "On Visiting the Sick," what advantages does a lower-income person have in dealing with sick people? Whatever your income, how can you build those advantages into your own life?

2. Describe what Søren Kierkegaard said was the one big difference between a human doctor and the Great Physician, Jesus?

3. How does the difference Kierkegaard describes affect our prayers for people who are ill and hurting? Or does it?

4. Wesley compared "The More Excellent Way" (love) to other, more visible gifts. Do you think we should pursue this "more excellent way" first? If we did, how would that

affect the way we serve? How could that affect the way we pray for the sick?

5. How did D. L. Moody explain the difference between our wills and God's? What did that have to do with answering prayer—even prayer for healing?

6. What is the big "if" Moody talks about in "Prevailing Prayer"? How do we deal with this big "if"?

7. In "The Gospel of Healing," A. B. Simpson explained why he thought prayer for healing cannot become a physical fountain of youth. Do you agree? Why, or why not?

8. What point is John Calvin trying to make in "Of Extreme Unction" by comparing oil to mud? If he's right, how does that affect us?

9. Do you agree with Calvin that the gift of special healing miracles was given to the original disciples of Jesus, and then not again? What's the difference between this view (which not all believers share) and his statement that "He cures our sicknesses . . . no less than he ever did"?

10. According to A. B. Simpson, at what point do we cross the line from persistent prayer to bothering God?

PART THREE

GRACE
TO LIVE

MARRIAGE

IT'S NOT HARD TO recognize the special regard God holds for the institution of marriage. So go ahead and search the Bible for the word *marriage* or *wedding*. You'll find practical advice in the Proverbs; poetic love songs in the Song of Songs; pictures of faithfulness with the prophet Hosea and his wayward wife, Gomer; ministry perspectives from the apostle Paul; and, of course, marriage as a picture of a larger relationship, of Jesus and his church. No wonder Jesus performed his first miracle at a wedding!

And no wonder marriage is under such attack today. Satan knows that if he can destroy marriage, the entire fabric of our society unravels. So more than ever, today's families need a shot in the arm. Only . . . where do we start?

Perhaps we begin with the basic instructions, as if we're planting a flower from the nursery. Whether a couple is celebrating their wedding day or their golden anniversary, what does a marriage need to stay healthy? Just like our other relationships, marriages thrive on accountability, mutual care, and submission to each other. As Christians, we no longer live alone, and the decisions we make in our relationships affect not only those we love, but also those who are linked to us in the larger body of Christ. That's why divorce, for example, has such a ripple effect throughout the church, and this may be part of the reason why God says in such explicit terms that he hates divorce.

There's a broader application as well. Even if we're single we can take the same practical techniques of respect or submission and apply those to any relationship we enjoy. Or we encourage families around us by the way we treat and support children, by the way we respect their parents. Thus our lifestyle choices affect those around us, which affect families, which affect marriages, which affect the strength of the body. As Romans 14:7 says, "None of us lives to himself alone and none of us dies to himself alone."

This is an important piece of wisdom to remember as we look for new and creative ways to strengthen marriages, families, and relationships in our own churches. We build from our own relationships, but let's take this family-strengthening exercise to the next level. Let's actively become part of the solution.

In the end, marriage in the church does not have to flounder, and it does not have to end in divorce. Church by church, we can begin to defy the odds. But it will take a lot of hard work, and it's going to take us out of our comfort zones. We begin by reading and understanding what wise people have said about marriage building.

Chapter 26

THE MARRIAGE OF CANA

GEORGE WHITEFIELD

Along with Jonathan Edwards and John Wesley, George Whitefield was one of the leading evangelists of the 1700s, traveling thousands of miles and crossing the Atlantic thirteen times between England and America. He was loved by many, including Benjamin Franklin, and is thought to have spoken to some ten million people. He met his wife-to-be, Elizabeth, while on a preaching tour in Wales; later their only child died as an infant.

In this message, Whitefield took a closer look at the marriage of Cana, where Jesus turned water into wine (John 2). Whitefield had much to say about the miracle and how it applied to Christians of the day, but also a bit about marriage itself.

Let's take it step by step. If Jesus went to a marriage feast, then it's clearly wrong to say that some people (priests, for example) must not get married. After all, the writer of the book of Hebrews says that "marriage should be honored" (13:4), and our Lord made a special point of performing his first miracle at a wedding feast.

What's more, God both designed and established marriage, even in the Garden of Eden before people sinned. So marriage is good for all people, including Christians who are brought closer to God through their faith in Jesus.

Why do we see so many unhappy marriages in the world, then? Because too many couples don't pray about their decision to marry, before it's too late. They don't go to mature believers for advice. Too often prayer is an afterthought at best. Even worse, the Devil has a hand in matchmaking that's built only on good looks or money. So no wonder those "weddings from hell" turn out to be miserable, grievous to the bone.

While I'm on the subject, let me say that the Devil's number one trap for young Christians is tempting them to jump into a lopsided relationship with an unbeliever, a person who is not born again. That's what happened before the biblical flood — in fact, it was one of the reasons why God sent the flood in the first place. What did Moses tell us about this in Genesis 6, verses 2 and 3? "The sons of God saw that the daughters of men were beautiful, and they married any of them they chose." Beautiful, maybe, but these young women didn't know God. And these men "married any of them they chose," not the ones God wanted for them, the ones God would choose. So what happened? "Then the LORD said, 'My Spirit will not contend with man forever, for he is mortal . . .'" In other words, even the people of God (and there weren't many) were taking the wrong road by marrying the wrong people, and it was affecting the entire world, turning it into a place that would have to be destroyed.

I might add that the ancient Bible leaders, the patriarchs, were very careful to choose wives for their kids out of God-fearing families. But when Esau rebelled against his father, one of the worst things he did was marry a Canaanite woman, since the Canaanites had nothing to do with God's promise.

That's about all I have time to mention on this subject. Let me just say, though, that if we want to marry, we should imitate the people of Cana in Galilee — by always calling Jesus to the marriage. He will always hear you and will direct you to the one who will support you the best in your spiritual walk. This is the kind of person who will help you serve Jesus without getting sidetracked. A person you can walk with and with whom you can please God, just like Zechariah and Elizabeth in the Bible. (See Luke 1.)

From George Whitefield, "The Marriage of Cana," a sermon preached in 1742, first published in *The Works of Reverend George Whitefield* (London, 1771–1772)

Chapter 27

IT'S NOT FOR SURE

CHARLES FINNEY

Charles Finney, the well-known preacher and revival leader, lived just a few years later than George Whitefield. The message that follows was delivered in New York sometime between 1836 and 1837. But he would have agreed 100 percent with Whitefield on one very dangerous trend at the time. Read on.

People are always telling me, "That's all fine, Pastor Finney. But even after everything you say, you have to admit these kinds of marriages aren't technically wrong. Right?"

Well . . . maybe. But when we read the Bible and look more carefully at the question of Christians marrying non-Christians, the general position that it's "not technically wrong" is shaky at best. In fact, the Bible clearly comes out against intermarriage with unbelievers.

Even if the Bible wasn't clear, though, what Christian ever married an unbeliever and didn't have doubts? The Bible says in Romans 14:23 that "everything that does not come from faith is sin."

So here are Christian men and women, moving ahead into relationships with unbelievers—and they're doubting the whole way. They say they're praying for guidance, but they're really hoping their conscience would just fade away. They're praying circles around God's command, and yet pressing on. Take care! Anybody who does this knows God's position, deep down. He forbids it. And don't forget that same verse in Romans 14 says that anyone "who has doubts [and still goes ahead with it] is condemned."

From Charles Finney, "Lectures to Professing Christians,"
a sermon preached in New York (1836–1837)

Chapter 28

THE MONK . . .
ON MARRIAGE

MARTIN LUTHER

I t's a unique story, set in early Renaissance Germany: Catholic
priest sours on the corruption and the abuses choking his church.
Sets out to debate theology, but the matter snowballs and the
priest is thrust into a position of leadership in a movement that eventually breaks off from the religious establishment. The Protestant
church is born. Later, Martin Luther decides to marry a former
nun, Katharina von Bora, and he has plenty of opinions on the
matter of Christian marriage, and how it affects the church. Here's
a sampling.

I have lots of other things to say, but I especially want to speak
up about how marriage as a whole has gone down the tubes.
You can go to any bookstore and pick up tons of pagan books
about how marriage is a total mistake and women aren't worth

it. I heard a Roman official who publicly told young men to go ahead and get married, but that was only because the country was always getting tangled up in foreign wars and they needed to eventually beef up the military.

The official, Caecilii Metellus, got heat from both sides of the issue. But eventually Roman public opinion concluded that women were a necessary evil, and that every family needs one. Incredible. Only blind heathens could come up with such nonsense. They have no idea that God created both men and women. Anybody who puts women down this way puts God down, since he created them. What are they thinking, that people just popped up out of nowhere?

I guess if women wrote more books, they'd be saying the same thing against men. But even if they didn't write it down, you can't miss their complaints.

You also can't miss how many parents today are discouraging their kids from getting married by telling them what a trial and a pain it is. By doing so they literally drag their children into a pit of evil. It's an ugly pattern, and God has to put up with this kind of grief—this rejection of his plan—all the time. The result? God allowed such people to reap what they sowed. In fact, he eventually gave them up to all kinds of mixed-up physical relationships, which Paul writes about in Romans chapter 1. Because people chose to slide so far into the gutter, God simply let them. Pagan books are chock-full of stories about people mired in such shameless lifestyles.

Naturally we don't want to go there; we want to live our lives as Christians. So start by holding on to this truth: Both men *and* women are God's work. Guard your heart and watch your mouth so you don't moan and complain about God's creation. When God called it good, we have no right to call it evil. He knows what's best for us, better than we do. That's why he says in Genesis 2:18 that "it is not good for the man to be alone. I will make a helper suitable for him."

There, see? God calls the woman *suitable,* a helper. If you don't agree, that's your own fault for not believing God's Word and work. This verse, this truth, is all it takes to come against anybody who's out to shipwreck marriage. And there are more than just a few.

On the flip side, young people need to be careful if they soak up non-Christian media or the anti-marriage talk on the street. They could be breathing poison. The Devil can't stand marriage, because it's God's will and God's work. That's why hell works so hard, shouting and writing against marriage any way it can. The Devil would much rather talk people into living outside of marriage, pulling them into a web of illicit sex and secret sin. Seems as if Solomon—though he had a lot to say to women who strayed from God's law—had the anti-marriage crowd in mind when he wrote in Proverbs 18:22 that "He who finds a wife finds what is good and receives favor from the LORD."

What is this good thing and this favor? Let's take a closer look.

We've all heard the saying "the honeymoon's over." That's how the world looks at marriage, as if the fun never lasts. Let them talk; people are bound to mock what God creates. They don't understand that marriage is much more than just saying "I do." See, if we're married but we don't understand the depth of what God intended, "marriage" will only make us bitter and turn into a total pain. Then, just like everyone else in the world, we'll be whining and complaining every chance we get.

The other side of the coin is the person who recognizes God's design for marriage, the Proverbs 18 kind of marriage, which leads to genuine joy and the deepest kind of lasting love.

How do we recognize God's marriage design? First, we have to believe that God invented marriage, that God brought one man and one woman together, and set up a process for them to have children and care for them. Check out God's Word on this—Genesis 1:28 says, "Be fruitful and increase in number."

So there. You can be sure that God never lies. You can also be sure that marriage and everything that goes with it pleases God. So tell me, how can a person find greater joy and delight than in God—particularly when we're 100 percent sure that our job description and our to-do list in life pleases God?

But how about this? Our natural instincts will sometimes take one look at married life and freak out. That inner voice says to us, "You've got to be kidding. I'm rocking the baby, changing diapers, making this kid's bed. Getting up in the middle of the night when that kid is screaming, putting that diaper rash ointment on. . . . And what is that smell? I didn't sign up for this kind of slave labor. If this is what being married is all about, I should have stayed single and free. In fact . . ."

What does Christian faith say to this? It opens its eyes and takes a close look at all the messy, smelly, little jobs that no one wants to do. The difference is that God's Spirit is like a pair of sunglasses, helping the Christian see things in a different light. In this light we can see God's stamp of approval on all the worst jobs. As if they're gold plated. Then the men can say, "Lord, I know you've created me as a man, and I know you've brought this child from my body—at least my part of the bargain. And because you're responsible for all this I know for certain that you're happy with the results. This is your perfect pleasure. But I confess I'm not worthy to take care of this little baby, or her mother. I'm not even worthy to rock this kid or change her diaper. So how do I rate? How did I come from being in last place to the point where I know I'm serving your creation and that I'm in the center of your precious will? I'm not sure, but I'll do this work, no matter how low and stinky it seems at the time. No matter what, nothing is going to keep me from this. Not earthquakes or tornadoes, floods or terror. Not if I lose my job . . . because I know beyond a shadow of doubt that this work pleases you."

A wife too should look at her duty to her family the same way, as she feeds her child, rocks and bathes him, or as she stays busy with other work, helping and supporting her husband. There's no doubt these jobs are gold. They're noble. In fact, the greatest good in married life is that God grants us children and tells us to bring them up to worship and serve him. Children make all the suffering and hard work worthwhile. That's because God is in the business of saving souls, and raising a family gives us a rich opportunity to join the work.

So Dad and Mom are apostles, bishops, and priests to their children, because parents introduce their kids to the gospel, the good news of Jesus. The bottom line is that there's no greater job in the world. It's a special privilege, since whoever teaches the gospel to another person is actually their apostle, their bishop. People might stumble on the accessories of power that church leadership can bring, but simply bringing the Word to kids produces true apostles and bishops. This is God's work and God's marching orders. It doesn't get any better!

Finally, though, I'd like to clear up one big objection to marriage. People say, "Sure, I wouldn't mind being married, but how can I afford it?" Yes, financial problems are the biggest obstacles to getting, and staying, married. Lack of finances are the biggest excuse for living together. Finances. What do I tell people? This kind of thinking shows a lack of faith. God can do more than we think. He's good, and he's true. Even so, I see people saying they want to have all their financial ducks in a row before they get married. Remember when Jesus said, "Do not worry, saying, 'What shall we eat?' or 'What shall we drink?' or 'What shall we wear?' For the pagans run after all these things, and your heavenly Father knows that you need them. But seek first his kingdom and his righteousness, and all these things will be given to you as well" (Matthew 6:31-33).

People with these questions want to pull their heads out of the noose of Genesis 3:19, the curse of sin that reminds us that "By the sweat of your brow you will eat your food." They'd rather ignore this truth and stay on vacation 24/7, and if they do get married they want to marry into money.

Forget it. Let these people do their own thing. Don't argue with them. It's not worth it. If it's a guy and he somehow manages to land a trophy wife, he's still going to be without faith and without Jesus. He's saying he trusts God—as long as he doesn't need him, anyway, or as long as his bank account is fat.

On the other hand, a real Christian shouldn't back away from being poor or looked down on. The believer shouldn't worry about doing jobs no one else wants to do, either. We should just take satisfaction in this: First, *that our status and our jobs please God.* Second, *that God will take care of us.* We just keep doing the best we can at what we're given to do. If we can't be a rock star or royalty, we can serve as a motel maid or a cafeteria worker.

See, God has already proven how he takes care of his people. Just look at the first chapter of Genesis. First he created and prepared everything we would need—including plants and animals—before he created us. That was just a demonstration of how God prepares all kinds of food and clothing for us, even before we need it. It's just up to us to keep working and not sit around waiting, and God is surely going to feed and clothe us.

On the other hand, unbelievers won't buy into this plan. They have to know that no matter how much they sweat over it, they can't magically produce a single grain of wheat in the field. They also know that even if their warehouses were full to the brim, they couldn't make use of a mouthful of food or a stitch of clothes, unless God gave them strength to live and breathe. They have to know this. But does it make any difference in the way they actually live?

Here's the bottom line on marriage: For those of us who aren't cut out for the long-term single life, we should make sure we keep busy first of all, and then that we get out there and find God's choice of mate. There's really no reason to wait too long. Let God worry about feeding us and our kids. Since God makes children, he's going to feed them too. If it turns out that God doesn't end up giving you a high-paying job and a lifestyle of the rich and famous, then don't sweat it. You can be happy that he's given you a Christian marriage, full of other blessings. Be thankful for what he's giving you here and now, and in the life to come.

From Martin Luther, "The Estate of Marriage"
(Wittenberg, Germany, 1522)

Chapter 29

SING EACH OTHER'S SONGS

WILLIAM BOOTH

William Booth, the founder of the Salvation Army, is best known for his dedication to evangelism and public service. The general's troops looked for the greatest needs, and rushed to meet them. They still do! But William and Catherine Booth also enjoyed a fruitful marriage of nearly forty years, a marriage of equals at a time when women's equality was still a matter of debate. In fact, Booth freely and fondly spoke of his wife often, in public and in print. So it was only natural after a few years that he answer some of his coworkers' questions about life, companionship, choosing a mate, even sex. He wrote down the best of his practical advice in a little book called Religion for Every Day. Here's an excerpt in answer to the question, "What makes a good marriage?"

As far as possible, sing each other's songs, love each other's friends, prefer each other's way of doing things, hold highly each other's goals. By doing that you'll help each other stay focused, energetic, and happy.

Don't forget that in a very real way, you're responsible for each other's souls, so it's up to each of you to handle this job faithfully. Here are a few practical steps:

First, don't hesitate to ask each other how you're doing spiritually. Maybe you do this with others (and you should). Why not with the one person who's closer to you than anyone else?

Second, make it your responsibility to look closely at how your spouse is doing with the Lord. Be loving and fair at the same time.

Third, pray for each other — together and separately.

Fourth, deal with each other's faults honestly, gently, and lovingly — the way you would want to be treated.

Fifth, take the time and the trouble to be your spouse's best coach, as well as cheerleader. Help each other grow closer to the Lord in a lifestyle that honors God and puts others first.

Be creative as you encourage each other to grow toward all-out dedication to God and his work for you. Because plenty of distractions and stumbling blocks are out there, things that would drag you away from serving him. Don't let Satan twist what should be the most beautiful relationship in the world — your marriage — into something that would steer you away from your first love: Jesus.

So push on together, and cheer each other on, especially

when you're depressed or discouraged. Those times will come. Let the other person know when you see him or her doing something right, and when each other's kingdom work could use a little improvement. But do it always in a spirit of love, in a way that no one else can.

Agree together on what you can give to others and to the work of the church. Remind each other of the promise you each made to serve God together. If you hit rough water and wish the Christian walk sometimes wasn't so hard, help the other person to keep faith! Your home and your children belong to God.

From William Booth, *Religion for Every Day* (New York: The Salvation Army Book Department, 1902)

Chapter 30

WITHOUT A CARE

CHARLES SPURGEON

Charles Spurgeon was easily England's best-known preacher for the last half of the 1850s. He started preaching when he was seventeen, then became pastor of London's New Park Street Church three years later. From 232 members, that church grew to become the largest independent congregation in the world. Spurgeon once addressed an audience of more than 23,000 people—all without amplification. But his most favored audience was his wife, Susannah, who was confined to bed and seldom was able to attend her husband's services. For her and for the rest of the congregation, he had much to say about relationships and marriage. Here's an excerpt from one of his famous sermons.

"I want you to live as free of complications as possible" (1 Corinthians 7:32, MSG).

When Paul first wrote these words he was trying to explain whether it was wise for Christians in those days to get married.

The question was whether they could be a better Christian if they were married or single. It was a sensitive question, and Paul gave such a clear answer. In the process he laid down a general principle that's even more valuable to believers today than was Paul's personal opinion about getting married or not.

Paul wrote that Jesus didn't give any specifics on the issue, but that he himself (Paul) had what he thought were sound opinions. In other words, no divine inspiration here—but I'd rather follow Paul's uninspired advice than anyone else's. He was sharper than anyone else you could name. You can bet the words were God-breathed when he explained his bottom line: "I want you to live as free of complications as possible." That's God's Holy Spirit talking just as sure as it is Paul. This piece of advice applies to our time just as much as Paul's. In fact, it's good for all time.

Let me flesh out the general idea. When we believe, we become servants of Jesus; we give up our own agendas. We're not our own; we're bought and paid for. (Check out 1 Corinthians 7:23 for more on this.) So our business in life is to serve the One who bought us, and that's a full-time job that should take all our time and energy.

Everything that helps us serve the Lord Jesus is a good thing, but everything that drags us down or keeps us from our main business in life is bad for us—even if it's fine for other people.

That's what Paul is trying to explain. On the surface, something might look fine for me to do, and it might be a completely acceptable thing to do. But (and this is the main point), if it keeps me from doing what God has called me to do, forget it! I have to pass it up.

If you want to be the best at something, you have to focus. That means giving up a lot of other things that are perfectly fine but take up the time and energy you need to excel at your one thing. The Christian walk is the same way. We need to tell ourselves, "I'm going to skip this because it won't help me serve God better. My job is to be in the best shape possible for serving the Lord."

Or the same with a soldier. Soldiers can't settle down, plant a crop, or take desk jobs. It's obvious: Even if there's not a war on, soldiers can't get bogged down in everyday life. Because when the alarm goes off and they're called to ship out, they have to be lean, mean, and ready to march—and the less baggage the better.

Just like the soldier, a Christian should aim to stay in shape, ready for holy warfare. A Christian can't be okay with answering the question of only, "Is this right or wrong?" We have a higher question: "Will this help me make God look better, or not?" It's a deeper question for a deeper Christian life, so we're careful to know the best answer.

Even the seemingly best thing is bad if it keeps us from our main goal as a believer. Even if our jogging sweats are embroidered with jewels and sewn together with gold thread, we're going to have to lay them aside if we're all about running to win. Our business is the prize, so we get rid of all the extra weight and the clothes that trip us up, so we can run the race.

Paul is saying to us that he wants us to live as free of

complications as possible. That means complications with things of this earth, so we can concentrate on things of heaven. He wants all our thoughts, cares, ideas, creativity, and burden-bearing to focus on our service to the Lord. After all, we have only so much brainpower and attention to invest, and he wants all of it for the Lord Jesus, so we can live like kids of the kingdom. Everything else? Live as free of complications as possible.

How does this work out in practical, everyday life? This is where the Holy Spirit comes in, because it's his work, really. Let's look more closely at how we cooperate with the Spirit's work.

First, to work in God's power, we steer clear of situations that we know will bog us down. Now, obviously, we don't choose where we grow up, that sort of thing. Sure, we're free to make life decisions at certain points, but sometimes we're thrown into life, and we just have to ride it out. Sometimes we're stuck in places that call us to struggle and grapple with life, and we can't get free. If God has placed a high hurdle before you, it's best not to leap over it. You may land in a ditch on the other side and end up worse than before. No, just cry out to God for help and trust in his sure Word. That way you'll be able to bear the burden he's put on you.

Even so, God allows us to choose at certain points in life, and that's where our Bible verse comes in.

Paul is talking about the marriage of Christians. First, he asks Christians not to marry, since that's a way to live as free of complications as possible. He said, when you're single "you're free to concentrate on simply pleasing the Master." On the other hand, he adds, "marriage involves you in all the nuts and bolts of domestic life and in wanting to please your spouse, leading to so many more demands on your attention."

Now take a look at the situation that led Paul to give this kind of advice. In those days Christians were hounded, dragged into court, thrown into horrible dark prisons, even fed alive to the lions in the stadiums, while people cheered.

All for being Christians.

It wasn't a great time for getting married and having kids. On the other hand, if you were single, you could flee if you needed to flee. Or if you were caught and were facing a death penalty for the crime of being a Christian, you didn't have to worry about leaving behind a spouse and kids. So the single person could pack lightly and hit the road for the gospel. Christian workers could minister in a town or city, and leave in a hurry if they needed to. They didn't need any help packing up a lot of things.

See? Paul wanted Christians to be more like an army, not weighted down with stuff. Paul himself carried around only what he needed for his tentmaking business—his sewing kit, a few needles, and a spool of thread—so he could work wherever he went. In this way he lived as free of complications as possible.

In those hard, desperate days, staying single was the best thing a young man or woman could do. Singleness put them in the best position to run, or suffer, or serve, or even . . . die. It just wasn't the time to settle down, start a business or farm.

That's the thinking behind Paul's recommendations.

We would give the same advice if times got tough again. But as a general rule, I'm not sure we should say such a thing today. Times are different, and we should follow the general principle rather than the specific application.

I've known fellow believers who were far more stressed out before getting married than after. They wanted someone to take care of them. I've known of women who were burdened as singles, only to find life much lighter after getting married. As married women they were able to serve God better and found themselves more free from stress.

So that's the general rule for marriage or singleness —whether you can serve God better, living free of complications. Problem is, too many of us don't look at the issue that way. Too many men and women rush into marriage even when they know that they will trade away their relationship with Christ, which will only keep them from really doing anything for him.

People often come to pastors asking for advice, when all they're really wanting is someone to rubber stamp what they've already decided. Still, I have to lay down the general counsel of Scripture, which every Christian man or woman has to accept. And this is it:

"I want you to live as free of complications as possible."

What's more, never forget that you don't belong to yourself, that Jesus bought you even though you were expensive. So as far as marriage goes, it's like everything else. Ask the Lord, "Will I be able to glorify and serve God better if I'm married . . .

or single?" And, "How can I best keep from raising my stress load and distract myself from serving the Lord?"

Obviously, good arguments exist both ways on this issue, but can you balance your life so you'll become a better servant of God . . . while married? If so, go ahead and marry. But if not, we shouldn't try to please ourselves at God's expense. We should not marry if we will not be at least as good a servant of Christ as before.

Because honestly, I've never met anyone who couldn't stand to improve as a servant. All of us could use a little help. So let's give our all to Jesus, and always remember Paul's plea:

Live as free of complications as possible.

From Charles Spurgeon, "Without Carefulness,"
a sermon delivered at the Metropolitan Tabernacle
(Newington, England, 1882)

PUTTING THE WORDS TO WORK

QUESTIONS FOR INDIVIDUAL OR GROUP STUDY

Use these questions as springboards for individual or group study.

1. In "The Marriage of Cana" George Whitefield paints a serious picture of what happens when believers marry unbelievers. Do you think he's overstating his case, or could it be a serious issue for today's church as well?

2. If Whitefield is right, how can the church today address this issue? What can we do?

3. What is Charles Finney saying about doubt in "It's Not for Sure"? And how does his point apply to marriage in the church today?

4. Were you surprised that a man in the 1500s talked about the equality of women? Based on what he said back then, how do you think Martin Luther would have regarded the status of women today?

5. What are some of the "messy, smelly little jobs that no one wants to do"? (Luther described several in "The Monk . . . on Marriage.") How do you feel when you have to do them? How can doing them bring you closer to God's design for your life?

6. Redefine the word duty without using any negatives. What does Luther have to say about the word in "The Monk . . . on Marriage"?

7. Describe Luther's take on money, wealth, faith, and marriage. How does it differ from your views? Would you feel comfortable counseling a young engaged couple the way he did?

8. Which of William Booth's tips for a good marriage ("Sing Each Other's Songs") is the hardest to take? Which, if followed, would make the biggest impact on marriages in your church?

9. Like the apostle Paul, Charles Spurgeon seems to think that lifelong singleness might not be a bad way to live. Is it possible to follow his advice in today's culture? Or do his words not depend on the way culture sees marriage?

10. Outside the married versus single debate, how can you apply Spurgeon's thoughts in "Without a Care" to your normal, everyday Christian walk?

VOCATION AND CHRISTIAN SERVICE

So we're saved. What next? God calls us to serve, so we look for ways to obey his command. The comforting thing is, *as God calls, he enables.* He doesn't say "do this for me" without giving us the equipment or the resources to succeed.

That's the message of Scripture and the theme of many of our finest, most passionate preachers and teachers. And though you can hear a lot of hard-hitting sermons and read plenty of how-to books on how to make a difference as a Christian, one of the best people to consult was a plain man named Dwight.

Here's a small-town boy who first came to the city to work in his uncle's shoe store. Often he would sit down with a rowdy group of young street kids, teaching them Bible stories and encouraging them to follow the Savior as he did. We know him as D. L. Moody.

Or Andrew, the missionary kid turned theologian. Though this South African pastor penned dozens of popular books on the deeper Christian life, he was best known by his family as being the father of eight children. Daddy. We know him as Andrew Murray.

Or Quintus, a sharp-tongued Roman lawyer, born in the African colonies and keen on advancing his career. As he watched how the persecuted Christians acted when the heat was turned up, though, he couldn't help himself. Quintus Septimius Florens Tertullianus gave his heart and his talents to the Savior. Today we know him as Tertullian, the early church father.

Or fifteen-year-old Charles, caught in a snowstorm and forced to seek shelter inside a roadside country chapel. That's where God got his attention, and his life would never be the same. The next year he would preach his first sermon, and he grew to become one of England's most famous preachers. We know him as Charles Spurgeon.

All of these men were from different generations in different parts of the world, but it seems they did share two passions. First, *reaching unbelievers for Jesus.* And second, *stirring up believers to serve him.* In doing so, they were following a pattern set down many years ago by Jesus and his disciples.

Is there a lesson here for today's Christians? Moody would think so, and he wasn't the only one. His approach: Find ordinary people with a heart for Jesus. Train them to become effective, ready witnesses for Jesus in all levels of society. Prepare and send an army of everyday believers to serve in their vocations around the world.

In this section we look closer at this view of service.

Chapter 31

TO EACH ACCORDING
TO HIS OWN ABILITY

ANDREW MURRAY

Most Christians have heard sermons on the parable of the talents. Here, though, Andrew Murray takes an in-depth look at how our service to God can more closely follow that familiar pattern. It's a fresh blueprint for Christian work assignments that we can all learn from!

The kingdom of heaven? "It's also like a man going off on an extended trip. He called his servants together and delegated responsibilities. To one he gave five thousand dollars, to another two thousand, to a third one thousand, depending on their abilities" (Matthew 25:14-15, MSG).

The parable of the talents shines a bright light on what our Lord Jesus teaches about the work he's assigned us. He starts with how he's gone to heaven and left his church in charge of his work on earth. He gives everyone something to do, no matter what gifts they've been given. He expects to get his investment back—with interest. Then he describes how badly the last servant blows his assignment, and what led to that disaster.

The parable says, "He called his servants together and delegated responsibilities," and that's literally what the Lord did in real life. He put his church in charge of all his work and goods. What are his goods?

- The riches of his grace (Ephesians 1:7)
- Spiritual blessings in heavenly places (Ephesians 1:3)
- His Word (Ephesians 6:17)
- His Spirit (John 14:26)

His servants receive all this, with all God's power, straight from the throne of God. It's a loan so we can do his work here on earth—the work Jesus began. It's like a businessperson leaving his hometown for a distant city, putting his business in the hands of employees he can trust. In the same way, Jesus made us partners in his work here on earth; he trusts it to us completely.

Of course, the work could go either way. The servant could neglect the work and it would fizzle, or put his heart into it and see it flourish. That's the bottom line of Christian service. To expand his kingdom, Christ depends on the faithfulness of his people.

The parable also says, "To one he gave five thousand dollars, to another two thousand, to a third one thousand, depending on their abilities." Yes, the assignments were different, but each servant got a share to take care of. So there's a direct connection between the grace God offers and the way he expects us to serve each other.

With that in mind, here's a truth we've almost lost: Every believer has been set apart to take an active part in winning the world for Jesus. No exceptions. Don't forget, Christ was a son first, then a servant. In the same way, every believer is a child of God first, then a servant.

Of course it's a child's highest honor to serve, for the father to trust him with his work. But the work of the church—here and overseas—will never be done the way it should be until every believer buys into the one and only purpose in life: working for the kingdom.

Back to the parable, where job one for the servants was to look after their master's business: "After a long absence, the master of those three servants came back and settled up with them" (Matthew 25:19, MSG).

Jesus isn't just going to settle accounts when he comes back to judge, he will check back on us frequently to see what we're doing and to make sure we're okay. He keeps a careful eye on the work he's given us, since his kingdom and glory depend on it. So he comes to approve and encourage—and to correct and warn.

Through his Word and his Spirit, God is also checking on us to make sure we're using our talents the way we should. He's seeing if we're dedicated and devoted to the work. If we are, we'll often hear, "Good work! You did your job well. From now on be my partner" (25:21, MSG).

If we're discouraged, he inspires us with new hope. If we're trying to do it all by ourselves, on our own steam and without his help, he sets us straight. But if we're asleep at the wheel or burying his investment funds, we're going to hear a tough warning: "I'm going to take away even the little bit he has" (see 25:29).

Christ's heart is in his work, and he's always keeping track with intense interest. So we must not let him down or fool ourselves, like the servant with the smallest share who "was afraid I might disappoint you, so I found a good hiding place" (25:25, MSG).

None of that. We need to learn two serious lessons from this servant. One, that he failed so miserably even though he had less to lose than the others. And two, that his master punished him severely for his failure. Taken together, this is a clear lesson for the church. We need to be extra careful, making a strong effort to teach the one-talent folks how to use their gifts. We need their service, too! Every branch needs to bear fruit—not just the branches of the strong, mature Christians. If a school is built on truth, every student gets the same attention—students who struggle, and students who excel.

It all goes to say that we must specially train even the weakest, most struggling believer. They need the opportunity to share the joy of serving Jesus, share the blessings that service brings. No one should be left behind when we're doing God's work.

Finally, remember what the servant thought of his master? He told him, "I know you have high standards and hate careless ways, that you demand the best and make no allowances for error. I was afraid" (25:24-25, MSG).

Enough. One of the biggest reasons we fail in Christian service? Misinterpreting God, thinking he's a tough taskmaster. If the church is ever going to bring the one-talent servants up to speed, if we're going to take care of the weakest brothers and sisters, we must get one thing clear: *God is all about grace and assurance.*

We also need to teach these people two things:

First, the Holy Spirit within them gives them all they need for the work to which God calls them. God himself strengthens them by his Spirit.

And second, doing God's work is full of joy, health, and strength.

Unbelief makes us lazy, but faith opens our eyes to see the blessings of working for God, how his strength is more than enough for us, and how serving Christ is well worth it.

Let's wake up, church! We have work to do, training up the weakest of our fellow believers to hear and respond to the call of Christ and his work. It's our job to bring them into the sold-out life for Jesus. That's true Christianity, the full measure of what it means to be saved.

From Andrew Murray, *Working for God*
(Grand Rapids, MI: Revell, 1901)

Chapter 32

WORK FOR EVERYONE

D. L. MOODY

Here's a short word from D. L. Moody on ministry and discipleship, originally delivered in 1877. Keep in mind that Moody was vitally concerned about Christian service and its effect on our Christian walk. (Notice his first comments.) To Moody, work was God's preferred instrument to grow us up.

Quite a few pages are coming loose in my Bible — sections I preach from the most. Mark 13 is loose, where it includes the verse, "To every man his work" (verse 34, KJV).

If we read this verse carefully, we find it doesn't say, "to every man some work," or "to every man a work." It says, "to every man *his* work." I believe that since eternity past God has laid out a work for every man and woman, so God has a plan for every person's life. What's more, no one else can do God's work for you or me. If we don't do our work, we'll surely answer to God. Notice it says in Romans 2:6 that "God will give to each person according to what he has done."

With that in mind, every one of us ought to take this question home with us: *Am I doing the work that God has for me?*

In the parable of the talents, the servant with two talents got the same reward as the one with five. He heard the same words: "Well done, good and faithful servant! . . . Come and share your master's happiness!" (Matthew 25:21).

Here's the thing: Those who take care of the talents God loans them always get more. But if we just bury our talent, God will take even that away from us. God doesn't want a person with one talent to do the work of someone with ten. All we must answer for is the talent God gives us.

Now, if we'd all do what God called us to do, don't you see how God's work would advance? I agree with what John Wesley said: "All at it, and always at it." We all have our own appointed task; no minister, elder, or deacon can do it for us.

Too many believers are weak and sickly, though, because they don't have these words carved on their hearts. It's bad news if your child stopped growing for ten or fifteen years, right? Well, that's exactly what's happening with many of God's children. I know some who are praying the same old prayers as they were twenty years ago. They haven't grown a spiritual inch in all that time.

The reason? They haven't done their work. It's that simple.

From D. L. Moody, *New Sermons, Addresses and Prayers*
(New York: Goodspeed, 1877)

Chapter 33

ON THE MINISTRY

TERTULLIAN

Tertullian, one of the outstanding early church fathers, used his training as a lawyer to powerfully defend the faith. His writings are important because of their place in church history. Taken as a whole, they're a picture of the larger church that early on slipped away from the grace of Christ and came to rely on a burden of good works. Tertullian struggled with the same issues, and in his later years slipped from grace to works. That burden within the church finally began to lift at the Reformation, but not until much later.

How is it that priests aren't allowed to do some of the things other Christians can? Everyone is a priest, because the Scripture says he "has made us to be a kingdom and priests to serve his God and Father" (Revelation 1:6). Only the church leadership has created a difference between clergy and the rest of us, and in some areas leadership has set the clergy apart for special honors.

But in areas that don't have this kind of nominating committee, you're able to lead worship and baptize on your own. You are your own priest! Anywhere three believers gather—even if none of them are ordained pastors—there's a church. As the apostle Paul told Roman believers, "God does not show favoritism" (Romans 2:11).

Of course, if you have a right as a Christian to be called a priest (in cases where there's a need), you also have to take on the responsibilities of a priest. It goes with the territory. So God's will is that we should all be fit and qualified to pass along his graces anytime, anywhere.

From Tertullian, in *De Exhotatione Castitatis 7,* quoted in
The Early Christian Fathers, ed. Henry Bettenson
(New York: Oxford University Press, 1969)

Chapter 34

SHE DID WHAT SHE COULD

D. L. MOODY

D. L. Moody preached many sermons weaving biblical examples with testimonies from his era. His goal? To give people a clear picture of the truth, and to help them put themselves into the shoes of these great examples in the faith. Oh, and then to motivate them to change! Here's a short example of how he used the well-known story of the woman who anointed Jesus with expensive perfume. Moody would have asked, "What's in this story for us today?"

Take a closer look at a line from Mark 14:8: "She did what she could."

If anyone had said back then that something was going to happen in Bethany that would outlast the Roman Empire, people would have sat up and taken notice. You'd see some excited people if they'd known this little event would outlive every member of royalty—past, present, or future. It would have attracted big crowds.

Of course, Mary had no idea she was about to erect a monument that would outlive empires and kingdoms. She never thought of herself, because love never thinks of itself.

Yet what did Jesus say in Mark 14? "I tell you the truth, wherever the gospel is preached throughout the world, what she has done will also be told, in memory of her" (verse 9).

So the story is mentioned in three separate gospel accounts: Matthew, Mark, and John. From there it's been told in hundreds of different languages, and now it's being published nonstop. There's even a society in London that prints five hundred records of this event, every working day. The story is being spread all over the world, and will be as long as God's church exists.

Some people try to erect monuments to themselves that will last long after they're dead and gone. On the other hand, this woman never gave monument-building a thought. All she wanted was to pour out her love on Jesus. What happened? Her act of devotion has been remembered through the years, and it will continue to be remembered as long as there's a church. It's as fresh today as it was a hundred years ago, even fresher now than five hundred years ago. In fact, the story has never been more well-known around the world, even though when Mary was alive she was unknown outside her hometown.

Kings have come and gone; empires have risen and

crumbled. The ancient glories of Egypt have passed away, and so has the once-mighty Roman Empire. Who knows the names of the dead people buried and embalmed in the pyramids? The wise men or mighty philosophers of Greece? Most of them are not exactly household names.

But the record of Mary's humble act continues to inspire us, over and over again.

Here's a common woman whose memory has outlived Caesars and conquerors. Although we don't know if she was wealthy, beautiful, or gifted, we do know she loved the Savior. She took a box of expensive ointment and broke it over the body of Christ. Someone once said it was the only thing Jesus received that he didn't give away.

Of course, in the eyes of the world the gift was no big deal. If there had been newspapers in those days, her actions would not have made the front page — maybe not even the paper at all. Yet this event has outlived anything else that happened during that time, aside from the other events connected with the life of Jesus.

How is this possible? Mary had Jesus in her heart, Jesus at the center of what she believed. She loved him and proved it by what she did.

Thank God every one of us can love Jesus the same way, and we can all do something for him. Maybe we'll do only little things, but if they're done for the love of Jesus . . . they'll last. They will outlive all the monuments on earth. See, iron and granite will rust and crumble. It will fade away. But anything done for Christ will never fade. Remember what Jesus said: "Heaven and earth will pass away, but my words will never pass away" (Matthew 24:35).

Here's the lesson from this Bible example: Every one of us can do something. If we're only willing to do what we can, the Lord will stoop down and use us. It's a great thing to be instruments in his hand.

And yet . . . maybe you still think you can't do much. So look at it this way: If God uses you to save one soul, that person may in turn be the key to saving a hundred more. Who knows? When I was in England about ten years back, I remembered a woman in the city we visited who got all fired up at the outreach meetings. It may even have been the same verse that moved her. ("She did what she could.")

In any case, this woman had been a Christian on the fringes for many years, and she never thought she had any particular mission in the world. I'm afraid too many professing Christians are in the same boat. But she got to the point where she began looking around for needs, seeing what she might do. She thought she would try to help needy young women out on the street. Her strategy? She just went out and started up conversations with the girls she met, offering them kindness and a listening ear. After a while, she rented a house, a place where they could get off the street.

When I returned to that city about a year ago, this woman had rescued over three hundred street people, restoring them to parents and homes. She still keeps in contact with each of them. Just think of all these sisters reclaimed from sin and death — all because of one woman.

She did what she could. Just think how she's going to jump and rejoice at the fantastic harvest, when she hears the Master say, "Well done, good and faithful servant."

From D. L. Moody, *To the Work! To the Work!* (Chicago: Bible Institute Colportage Association, 1896)

Chapter 35

WANTED: VOLUNTEERS!

CHARLES SPURGEON

Charles Spurgeon was very much like his contemporary D. L. Moody in appeals to his audience. Spurgeon was never satisfied unless he gave his audience a practical way to apply biblical truth and to get involved with spreading the good news of Jesus. Here's a perfect example of Spurgeon's approach to discipleship, his belief in putting ordinary people to work building the kingdom.

Here's an important observation, although it might not seem so at first. When a soldier named Amasiah willingly offered himself to the Lord (2 Chronicles 17:16), *he did it in a secular calling.* After all, Amasiah wasn't working in a church or a Christian ministry.

He also didn't say that he had to be a prophet, or else he wouldn't serve. I'm not sure why, but sometimes when a certain kind of young man gets the idea to serve God, he usually wants to talk with me about how he can get into "the ministry."

I take a look at one of these guys, and sometimes it's clear his mouth was never made for preaching. His eyes weren't made for looking a congregation in the face. When he starts to talk, I get the impression that he might make a good learner for the next twenty years, and after that maybe he might be up for teaching Sunday school. Maybe.

Some people just don't have the gift of teaching—but that should never keep them from serving the Lord. Remember, we didn't hear Amasiah say, "Lord, I'm going to give myself to you, as long as you make me a headliner act—a prophet."

Not at all! Amasiah willingly offered himself to the Lord, to be and to do whatever the Lord wanted him to be and to do. So he remained a soldier. After all, he was in the army, he never went to college, and we don't know that he ever preached a sermon in his life. Even so, says the Bible, he "volunteered himself for the service of the LORD," he willingly offered himself to the Lord.

You can volunteer for the Lord's service as a shoe repair worker. You wouldn't be the first consecrated cobbler, by the way. Or you could willingly offer yourself to the Lord even as you work your nine-to-five job cleaning chimneys. After all, people need their chimneys cleaned. Though your face gets dirty, your heart can stay clean.

Or you might be working on a road crew, handling crushed rock, praying that the Master would break stony hearts around you. A person can serve the Lord while working at any legitimate business. It's a terrific privilege and blessing to work at winning souls, but we shouldn't separate that work from everything else in life, as though evangelism was the only sacred work, and everything else was almost a sin.

Serve God where you are. But how?

Well, if you're home watching kids, you're serving God by bringing them up to know Jesus. May God help you to do it! Or if you're helping your mom, don't worry about moving the world just yet. Be happy moving the bed when you make it tomorrow morning.

Plenty of folks who have grandiose plans for "Look at me!" glory will end up serving God best by doing common work in a common place. Maybe God will keep them at that work—at least until they get back down to earth and get their heads on straight.

In any case, it must have been tough for Amasiah to live all out for God as a soldier. He had a tough calling, but tough or not, he did it. So wherever you find yourself, serve God where he's called you. Glorify God in whatever work you have, just like Amasiah.

As Paul told the Corinthian church, "He who was a slave when he was called by the Lord is the Lord's freedman; similarly, he who was a free man when he was called is Christ's slave" (1 Corinthians 7:22).

Even if you're stuck in the barracks, be bold to talk about the God you serve. Many people have even come to the Lord after seeing a fellow soldier praying. But the bottom line is this: Don't forget the example of our spiritual heroes, in and out of the army. They remind us that no matter how tough the job, God's grace will carry us through—just as it did with Amasiah.

> From Charles Spurgeon, "Wanted! Volunteers," a sermon
> delivered at the Metropolitan Tabernacle
> (Newington, England, March 22, 1891)

Chapter 36

SERVING THE LORD

CHARLES SPURGEON

Charles Spurgeon did much to spur his people on to serve God as he preached from the pulpit of the Metropolitan Tabernacle. Here's a short example of his straight-shooting, no-nonsense approach to discipleship and service. Notice he's not afraid of stepping on anybody's toes!

If we truly want to serve God we need to follow his directions, period. Wouldn't you be irritated if you hired a housekeeper, but all she did was constantly run up and down the stairs, wander through all your rooms, open and shut the closet doors, dust and rearrange furniture here and there, and basically just flitter around? You wouldn't call this service. You'd just be annoyed.

So if we're charging ahead without orders, we may be keeping busy, but we can't call it service. If we don't follow orders, we're disobeying—plain and simple. Brothers and sisters! How many of us think we're serving God when we've never even looked in the rule book, never paid attention to the great King's commands, recorded in his Word?

Maybe we think we're worshiping God, but we've invented something on our own. We think it's great because it's creative. Or we think it's proper because it's been done this way before. Or, even better, because it's been done this way for a long time. Problem is, we forget that God's Word is the only standard, and service isn't service unless it's commanded from Scripture. Why don't more Christians see this? They load themselves down with busywork, but God doesn't even want most of it. In fact, Christians have simply invented most of it.

Please ask yourselves this question, friends: How do you set your agendas? Who fills your calendars? Who decides what to write on your to-do list? I ask myself the same questions, and it comes down to this: *Are we listening to the Master?* Are we asking ourselves, "What does he really want us to do?"

Otherwise, it's so easy to get pulled down the stream of church activities, drowned in tradition, and never serve the Lord truly. Or you might be busy doing your own thing, your universe revolving around "me first." Those kinds of efforts won't serve God, either, since you never asked what *he* wanted first.

As disciples, we bow our necks and hitch up to the harness of Christ. Just like the best service employees, we always have our eye on whom we serve—Jesus. He lets us know what he wants, and what he wants for us. Whatever the king orders, that's what we do. But if he doesn't tell us to do something, it's not our concern, even if popes and the highest archbishops want it done.

So do you listen to the King's wishes? Here's an example: Have you obeyed his command to be baptized? Believer's baptism is clearly called for in Scripture, but I'm afraid some of you know exactly what you need to do . . . and don't do it. So I'm praying the Holy Spirit will show you the sin of ignoring God's command as he turns you around to go the right way. Our will must bow, our heart obey.

Otherwise we'll never be serving the Lord.

From Charles Spurgeon, "Serving the Lord,"
a sermon delivered at the Metropolitan Tabernacle
(Newington, England, August 15, 1869)

PUTTING THE WORDS
TO WORK

Use these questions as springboards for individual or group study.

1. In "To Each According to His Own Ability," Andrew Murray mentions "goods" several times. Which "goods" has the Lord given you? How do you know? And how can you use them?

2. Who is more qualified for service in the church? Those with several talents, or fewer? Why?

3. Why do we often fail in Christian service, according to Murray? What can we do to change that?

4. Describe the relationship between work and Christian maturity, as D. L. Moody described it in "Work for Everyone."

5. Do you have any pages loose in your Bible, pages loosened from overuse? If not, why not?

6. According to Tertullian ("On the Ministry"), what's the definition of a "priest"? Could you ever be one? Why would you want to be?

7. What kind of monument does Moody favor in "She Did What She Could"? How can you build one?

8. Who do you know who might be a living monument? What have they done to be considered one?

9. According to Charles Spurgeon in "Wanted: Volunteers!" what's the difference between just working a nine-to-five job and working for the Lord? What are the necessary ingredients? Do you have them in your work? If not, how can you get them?

10. In "Serving the Lord," Spurgeon talks about orders. What are yours?

IN CLOSING

WHAT DO WE DO now with so much good advice?

The answer to that question will determine if this book, in the end, was worth your time. It's easy to read these chapters and see the truths swim past, lost in the blur of last week's sermon, next week's Sunday school lesson, and something we heard on the radio. We're not the only ones who wrestle with information overload.

In the process, this book can sit on the shelf, like so many other nice books with nice messages, or we can use it as a blueprint for renewal.

So we return to this ancient concept, the sacraments, this graceful pattern for church life. Ours? Most believers would like to follow God's intentions for baptism and communion. For discipleship and reconciliation, as well. For healing, or for our marriages. And for our vocations—what we do with our life's work. My prayer is that this book will provide enough of a framework to help us navigate our way back to what God intends for our lives, what God intends for our churches. It's a voyage of rediscovery, back through God's grace.

Don't forget, though, that God's best gifts will permeate our lives only with our permission, with our active consent. It's fitting, then, that we close with a last bit of advice from one of our contributors, Andrew Murray, taken from the introduction to his devotional classic, *The Lord's Table*:

Please don't settle for just reading the day's entry, then close the book and leave it at that. Take time to really think about it and look for ways to plug it into your own experience.

It will take time, though. Your time. I'm convinced that some people don't grow in their walk with God because they don't spend time with him in private prayer. After all, we can't download instant spiritual truth. It just doesn't work that way. Because even though I might understand (and agree with) what I read, it'll normally have a short shelf life in my memory. Unless, of course, I take time to focus on the reading quietly and in private. That gives it a better chance to soak in, to actually become a part of my thinking.

So give God time to transfer his thoughts into your inner, spiritual life. After you've read a section, sit quietly before him . . . and stay there until he brings his words to life in your soul. As you do, you'll notice the life power he gives.

Which brings me to my second point: Don't be steered away from God's Word by other sources—

even useful books that point to the truth. Because if we get all our information and teaching from talking heads or commentators, it's always secondhand. We'll get used to it that way. A book like this is useful only if it leads us right back to God's Word, where we can meditate on the truth straight from God's mouth.

Don't forget—God's Word is packed with incredible power, with many hidden blessings we can't even get our minds around. So be sure of this: When you read this book always check back to the Scripture references.

—Andrew Murray, introduction to *The Lord's Table*
(Grand Rapids, MI: Revell, 1897)

To that I can only say, Amen.

ABOUT THE AUTHOR

ROBERT ELMER is a graduate of Simpson College and St. Mary's College in California. Most recently he is the author of *Practicing God's Presence: Brother Lawrence for Today's Reader* as well as over forty popular novels for younger—and older—readers. He and his wife, Ronda, are the parents of three young adults and live in Idaho. Visit his website at www.RobertElmerBooks.com.